Kriya Yoga

With unceasing blessing
Paramahansa Yogananda
April 8th, 1950

Kriya Yoga

Spiritual Awakening for the New Age

Nayaswami Devarshi

CRYSTAL CLARITY PUBLISHERS Commerce, California

CRYSTAL CLARITY PUBLISHERS
1123 Goodrich Blvd. | Commerce, California
800.424.1055 | crystalclarity.com
clarity@crystalclarity.com

ISBN   978-1-56589-112-8 (print)
ISBN   978-1-56589-598-0 (e-book)
Library of Congress Cataloging-in-Publication Data
    2022055954 (print) | 2022055955 (e-book)

Cover design by Tejindra Scott Tully
Interior layout and design by Michele Madhavi Molloy

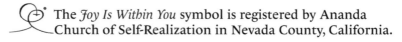

The *Joy Is Within You* symbol is registered by Ananda
Church of Self-Realization in Nevada County, California.

Contents

Foreword

You're about to read a book that can transform your life. Kriya Yoga is much more than the latest theory for self-improvement, but is based on an ageless tradition of universal truth: the ancient science of yoga and meditation.

Yes, "ancient" because its roots go back in time to a period long before historical records were kept. Stone seals showing people seated in various yoga postures have been found in the Indus Valley of India, and have been dated by archaeologists as far back as 5000 B.C.

And, yes, "a science" because its assumptions have been tested in the laboratory of human life and consciousness over millennia and have proven to be true. In fact, modern researchers in such highly-respected institutions as Harvard Medical School and the Mayo Clinic have been doing extensive studies on the effects of meditation. Their findings show that a regular practice lowers blood pressure, improves the quality of sleep, improves concentration, reduces stress, controls anxiety, and reduces age-related memory loss, to name a few.

But the greatest benefit of Kriya Yoga, which is a technique of meditation, is the positive transformation it brings in our own consciousness. Through Kriya practice, we become aware of an untapped reservoir of subtle energy within us. By learning to direct this energy to higher centers of consciousness in the brain, we begin to experience our own highest potential.

We can say this from personal experience, since we've been practicing Kriya for more than fifty years. The clarity and peace of mind, increased capacity to love and understand others, and the ability to deal calmly with challenges are priceless gifts. Perhaps most important is that over time we begin to experience ourself as a part of a greater reality that underlies everything.

Nayaswami Devarshi has presented Kriya Yoga in an easily understandable and engaging way. This book is filled with inspiring, thought-provoking stories from his own life and those of others. Such a presentation of Kriya for the general public has long been needed, and is a great contribution to the understanding of how human consciousness evolves.

Another major theme convincingly presented here is that we are entering a New Age, called by the sages of India, *Dwapara Yuga*. According to this teaching, our planet is moving from a time in which fixed, separate forms and material thinking were considered the norms. This materialistic approach is still reflected in many entrenched religious, political, and national institutions.

Dwapara Yuga is characterized by fluid, unitive thinking and seeing things not in terms of form, but of energy. This kind of thinking can be seen in many cutting edge developments in science, business, and human relationships. Because Kriya Yoga works by awakening inner energy and the resultant fluidity of thought, it may be said to exemplify the consciousness of this new age.

This book may open doors for you that lead to greater happiness, inner freedom, and Self-awareness. As each of us transforms our own consciousness, we can also help bring about a change in the world around us. As Mahatma Gandhi so eloquently said: "You must be the change you wish to see in the world." Through sincere practice, Kriya Yoga holds the key to personal and global upliftment.

Nayaswami Jyotish
Nayaswami Devi

Introduction

In **August 1920,** a young Paramhansa Yogananda, author of *Autobiography of a Yogi*, set out on the long ocean voyage from his native India to America, bringing with him the ancient teachings of meditation and Kriya Yoga.

When asked, "Is your teaching a new religion?" Yogananda replied, "It is a new *expression* of truths that are eternal."

His simple words refer to *Sanatan Dharma*, the eternal truth which predates all religions.

Yogananda declared, "You are on the eve of a great spiritual awakening, a great change in the churches, where true souls will be drawn to seek the experience of God's presence."

Formal religion focuses mainly on outward rituals, dogmas, and rules, and on the false notion that the worshiper can only approach God through the intercession of a priest. Yogananda called such religion — equally common East and West — "Churchianity."

Yogananda's teacher, Swami Sri Yukteswar, explained that the planet has entered into a new age. He wrote that we have exited *Kali Yuga*, an age of materialism and outward form. Only recently has the planet moved into

Dwapara Yuga, an age of energy, growing awareness, and fluidity. Modern science has shown that matter *is* energy.

Every significant invention of the twentieth century is based on the new energy-awareness, from telegraphs, telephones, and radios, to countless electronic technologies and gadgets that have fundamentally changed people's lives.

A new understanding is similarly growing in spirituality and religion. Many people now question the purpose of outward forms and rituals—they seek instead the direct inner experience of higher truth.

Yogananda dedicated his life to showing *how* to have that direct personal experience. Essential to his mission was introducing the ancient teachings of Kriya Yoga and writing fresh interpretations of two of the great world scriptures, the Bhagavad Gita and the Bible.

Kriya Yoga (which I will often refer to as "Kriya") is more than a technique. Yogananda gave the technique of Kriya to his students as part of a comprehensive way of life, designed to help them individually realize their soul natures—and to bring that realization into their daily lives.

Millions would learn about Kriya Yoga from Yogananda's *Autobiography of a Yogi*, published in 1946. I was surprised to read that Kriya, or a similar technique, was taught by Krishna to his disciple Arjuna, by Christ and his disciples, by the Indian sage Patanjali, and by many other enlightened teachers over the centuries.

"The Science of Kriya Yoga," a central chapter in his autobiography, bridges the divide between science and religion. The yoga science is based upon universal inner realities. Two simple examples: someone sitting upright with a straight spine will feel more energy than someone sitting slumped over; someone whose eyes are gazing upward will feel more uplifted than someone looking down. These responses come regardless of our religious beliefs.

Meditation is also an art. The highest expression of any art, such as painting or music, is much more than demonstration of technique. Great artists work with feeling and intuition. Perfect technique alone never makes an artist's works great. Nor can spiritual techniques alone, including Kriya Yoga, make someone a saint, one who has realized God.

In *Autobiography of a Yogi*, Yogananda recalls his boyhood meeting with a great yogi-saint, Bhaduri Mahasaya, who said to him:

> "You go often into the silence, but have you developed *anubhava* (actual perception of God)?" He was reminding me to love God more than meditation. "Do not mistake the technique for the Goal."

The saints of all traditions are living canvases demonstrating the highest human art and science.

Paramhansa Yogananda predicted a bright future for humanity: a future with a unitive understanding of the shared reality that connects us all. That understanding will lead to fulfilling Yogananda's broader mission, to "inspire the nations to forsake suicidal wars, race hatreds, religious sectarianism, and the boomerang-evils of materialism."

He commissioned a direct disciple, Swami Kriyananda, with showing how his teachings could shed light on every aspect of human existence. The monastic name, *Kriyananda*, is unusual in the Indian tradition—Kriya means "action" and "ananda" means "divine bliss." Thus "Kriyananda" means "one who strives to realize the bliss of his nature through right action, including the practices of Kriya Yoga."

Swami Kriyananda dedicated his life to showing how to apply the teachings of *Sanatan Dharma* and the practices of Kriya Yoga to every aspect of life. The Ananda communities he founded are living laboratories of this practical science and art. They are proof that a spiritual life can create bonds of harmony and cooperation between souls from all religious, cultural, and national backgrounds.

This book is the fruit of more than forty years of personal experience of the Kriya path and teachings, most of which have been devoted to sharing them with others.

Whether you are already a practitioner of Kriya Yoga or wish to learn more about Kriya, I hope this book will give you a better understanding of its depth and breadth. If you follow another spiritual practice, I believe the universal principles of Kriya can help shed light on your path.

— NAYASWAMI DEVARSHI

Humanity during *Dwapara Yuga* will cease to depend on crystallized political and institutional systems and will seek more fluid definitions of its ideals. In the past three centuries we have seen the wane of organized religion—of "Churchianity," as Yogananda called it—and an increasing affirmation of the inner spirit of religion. Religion used to be identified with church affiliation and formal statements of belief; now it is becoming identified with inner Self-realization, and with a less structured, more informal fellowship of truth-seekers with one another.

— SWAMI KRIYANANDA

Kriya Yoga

Spiritual Awakening
for the New Age

CHAPTER ONE

Kriya Yoga:
Spiritual Awakening for the New Age

Outward ritual cannot destroy ignorance because they are not mutually contradictory.

— PARAMHANSA YOGANANDA, *Autobiography of a Yogi,*
QUOTING ADI SHANKARA FROM HIS *Century of Verses*

I was raised in a religion that featured primarily outward rituals. My experience is, I suspect, true for many people living today, whatever their religion. Perhaps you, dear reader, share my early lack of enthusiasm for performing practices to an unknowable God somewhere "up there." I was unconvinced by the promise of an unseen heaven and future salvation, given as a reward for following that religion.

As a child, the ways of this world seemed foreign to me. I was fortunate to have an identical twin brother who shared my otherworldly perspective. I still delight in the memory of the summers we spent roaming the vast forest just behind our home. When it came time to enter kindergarten, we were horrified by the prospect of being caged in school rooms for years of formal education. When the dreaded day arrived, we supported each other in refusing to enter school. Of course, we were forced to face the inevitable, though we stubbornly held out for several days.

The church we were raised in, the Catholic Church, seemed more mystifying than enlightening. We attended from a sense of duty, fulfilling our obligations until our teen years, when we simply walked away. Only after learning meditation was I able to feel a profound, renewed appreciation for the saints and some of the practices I'd been brought up in.

I never stopped wondering why we were born into this world. I knew that there was much more to life than getting an education, finding a career, raising a family, and regular church attendance. Many young Americans in the 1960s and 1970s began asking the same questions that troubled my brother and me. I'm pleased to see many people revisiting the same questions today.

During the widespread spiritual awakening of the 1960s, many wonderful books appeared, written by or about great saints in East and West. Reading about meditating yogis who practiced an inward way of finding truth and God, I finally began to find answers.

I was particularly stunned to read about yogi saints and Christian saints on the very same pages! One book described their shared experience of the divine as the same truth—not as something "out there," but as the unfathomable joy of God that is within each of us.

I must have been about seventeen when I found myself walking along a forest trail one day—the same forest that had seen many summers of childhood play. Awakened by my reading, by the peaceful environment, and surely by seeds sprouting from long-forgotten lifetimes, I had a spontaneous and overwhelming experience of joy.

I *knew* at that moment, "*This* is what the saints and yogis are talking about! This bliss *is* God!"

A particularly sweet moment came during my joyful wandering when I observed an elderly black man fishing in a lake. Even though separated by age, race, and now religion, I felt a transcendent bond of divine love for him, even *with* him—a love that could only be from God.

I had to resist the impulse to share my great discovery with him, of who and what we really are—a Truth that I understood at the very core of my being: that we are all made of the same divine love and bliss about which the great saints and yogis have spoken since the dawn of time.

I took a solemn inward vow at that moment: "I will spend the rest of my life as a yogi seeking God!"

Bear in mind that I had never met a yogi at that point! I also had no idea how one would spend a life seeking God as a yogi in America, or where I could find a yogi. I'm sure that if I had shared my thrilling discovery with my high school career guidance counselor, he'd have taken me off to a psychiatric facility!

The truth of my experience was confirmed a few years later when I read Paramhansa Yogananda's *Autobiography of a Yogi*. I was thrilled to read the story of how Yogananda achieved the goal of his lifelong search: the experience of union with God—it was vastly greater than my own first glimmering divine perceptions. He spoke of the experience as "*samadhi* bliss."

Soon after that experience, he asked his guru, Swami Sri Yukteswar, "When will I find God?"

His Guru replied:

> "I am sure you aren't expecting a venerable Personage, adorning a throne in some antiseptic corner of the cosmos!
>
> "*Ever-new Joy is God*. He is inexhaustible; as you continue your meditations during the years, He will beguile you with an infinite ingenuity. Devotees like yourself who have found the way to God never dream of exchanging Him for any other happiness; He is seductive beyond the thought of competition."

Years later, my newfound understanding of the unity between the saints of different religions was confirmed by a story told by Swami Kriyananda in his autobiography, *The New Path: My Life with Paramhansa Yogananda*:

> In St. Louis one day Master [Yogananda] visited a Roman Catholic monastery. The abbot had seen Yogananda in meditation and knew him for a great saint. The other monks were horrified

to see this orange-robed 'heathen' in their midst. When the abbot arrived on the scene, however, he hastened over and embraced Paramhansaji lovingly. 'Man of God,' he cried, 'I am happy you have come!'

The saints alone are the true custodians of religion. For they draw their understanding from the direct *experience* of truth and of God, and not from superficial reasoning or book learning. The true saints of one religion bow to the divinity manifested everywhere, including of course to the true saints of other religions.

Our planet has entered a time of extraordinary transition — a time when that universal truth is becoming more and more self-evident. Sri Yukteswar (Yogananda's guru and guide) wrote about the change in our planetary cycle from one epoch, *Kali Yuga*, to the next, called *Dwapara Yuga*. In his book, *The Holy Science*, he describes this time as the dawn of a more enlightened age, when many souls will awaken spiritually.

This ascending cycle explains the timing of Yogananda's life's work: bringing Kriya Yoga and an inner understanding of religious and spiritual practices. The sweeping planetary changes account for a growing worldwide interest in meditation. It is also the catalyst for the rapid change we see in the world, change that becomes conflict when old understandings resist the new.

A commonly accepted belief in India is that we are still in the dark age of *Kali Yuga*. Sri Yukteswar persuasively resolved this confusion, basing his conclusions on astronomical considerations and observable progress in science, technology, and human evolution. Signposts described in ancient texts are corroborated by abundant evidence that we are in an ascending age: a longer human life span; people growing taller from generation to generation; greater intelligence; and greater awareness of energy.

We are still very early in the long evolution from the darkest age to the most enlightened, but the tide has turned. If you would like to learn more about these long cycles of time, I highly recommend *The Yugas: Keys to Understanding Man's Hidden Past*, by Joseph Selbie and David Steinmetz.

Kali Yuga was an age of materialism and form, where matter and structure were the commonly perceived reality. The great rays of energy of *Dwapara Yuga* will, in time, melt the frozen forms of that older age, though not without a struggle. We can see centuries-old social, economic, and religious structures eroding and sometimes failing altogether. People everywhere are being challenged to re-examine their lives and redefine their understanding of the world, including their relationships and their religious beliefs and practices.

Yogananda came as a way-shower to help bring civilization proactively into this new age. The inward practices of Kriya Yoga are key to helping humanity integrate an enlightened inner life into every aspect of outer life.

Kriya is not restricted to those who have renounced family, business, or worldly life. During the so-called Dark Ages, those who pursued an inner life would generally have to flee from the powerful materialistic vibrations of the age in order to pray and meditate. We no longer need to turn away and hide in order to find God.

This new age is the catalyst for change in every aspect of life:

1. Religious and spiritual practices will focus on inner growth

There will still be rituals—they *do* have a place in the spiritual life—but they will be more and more informed by direct inner experience. The outward practices of old traditions only hint at, sometimes even *hide*, the inner truth. In such practices, the priest keeps the seeker at arm's length from God. In the new age, spiritually minded people are beginning to worship inwardly in their meditation rooms or in group meditation with others. This inward worship is performed, in Yogananda's words, on the "altar of the Spirit" within.

Science, too, has begun to prove the efficacy of inward practices that help still the mind, calm the agitated emotions and anxieties, and open the heart.

2. There will be a growing awareness of energy, the importance of having more energy, and gaining control of that energy

Yoga and meditation practices have long included techniques for controlling the inner life force. The Sanskrit word for that control is *pranayam*. In *Kali Yuga*, people thought *pranayam* meant only "breathing exercises." Such is still a common view. The dawning age of energy is bringing in the understanding that *pranayam* is a *condition*—that of *having* control over our energy, emotions, and thoughts.

Pranayam can also refer to those techniques that help us to control the inner energy, or *prana*.

3. Individuals will take responsibility for developing a relationship with God

I remember hearing a popular comedian wryly point out that "studies show thousands of people are leaving the churches . . . and going back to God!" Many people have abandoned formal religion but still consider themselves spiritual seekers—and are even more dedicated in their seeking than when they were churchgoers. Increasingly, spiritually minded people will understand that church or religious membership cannot, by itself, help us to know God.*

4. There will be many new types of religious movements and an evolution of traditional religions

Yogananda once called his movement a "Church of All Religions." He wrote and spoke at length about the *original teachings* of two great world religions—Christianity and Hinduism. He said, "Jesus Christ was crucified once, but his teachings have been crucified daily since then by millions who claimed to be Christians." He spoke in the same vein about distortions in the teachings of all the great world religions.

5. There will be a growing awareness that religion based solely on a masculine or patriarchal God is only half true

In *Kali Yuga*, most religious traditions worshiped a

---

* A prominent study in 2017 found that over a quarter of all Americans consider themselves "spiritual but not religious."

masculine God, had male priests, and an outwardness that is a predominantly masculine trait. Mostly absent were the qualities more traditionally associated with the feminine aspect of the Divine: receptivity, love and devotion, compassion, and kindness. These are the very qualities the world needs now in order to restore the balance that was lost during *Kali Yuga*.

Swami Kriyananda spoke to a large American audience of the need, in this age, to tune in to the aspect of God as the Divine Mother, just as Paramhansa Yogananda worshiped God in Her form as the Divine Mother.

6. Religious organizations will put the needs of the individual first

No longer will religious organizations put institutional needs above the spiritual welfare of their members. Just as individuals can develop spiritual pride, so can organizations, their leaders, and their followers. In the new age, organizations will grow and thrive if they understand their primary role is to support people in their individual relationship with *God*—rather than in their relationship with the *church*.

7. Individuals will develop a unitive understanding of life and the underlying reality that connects us all

An inward spirituality naturally awakens a transcendental awareness of a much greater reality, a reality that unites all souls. That unitive understanding will someday "inspire the nations to forsake suicidal wars, race hatreds, religious sectarianism, and the boomerang-evils of materialism," as Yogananda wrote in his autobiography. It will usher in a new era of respect and love for the presence of God in every person, every tree, plant, river, mountain, and animal—in all of creation.

This transition will not be without challenges, challenges even now dramatically demonstrated in our world. The old forces of *Kali Yuga*, though on their way out, are enlivened by the increasing energy of the new age. With this infusion of energy the old ways are putting up a last fight for survival—a fight that for all its present turmoil is only a passing phase. As heat melts ice into water and then into vapor, so the increased energy of this new age will dissolve the old rigidities.

We will gain the most by cooperating with the new ray of energy. We can visualize this energy as a powerful wave sweeping the world. Those who resist it will be overcome and swept away. Those who learn how to ride the wave, much like a surfer on the ocean, will find their spiritual progress greatly accelerated.

If you are feeling discouraged by the short-term trends in religion, politics, institutions, and society, take heart! Yogananda assured us that *Dwapara Yuga*, the age of energy, will have the final word.

We have emerged from *Kali Yuga*—a male-dominated era when physical force seemed the only way of attaining one's objectives—and are already being swayed by the fresh spring breezes of *Dwapara Yuga*, the Age of Energy. There will be increasing awareness of the need for feminine inwardness as a balance to masculine outwardness; for inner inspiration as a balance to outward conquest; for feeling, as the very essence of consciousness itself. In the struggle to adapt to these changes, it will be increasingly necessary to distinguish between calm feeling, which is intuitive, and the disruptive feelings of raw emotion. There is a need—now, today—to recognize the importance of inner peace as the soil in which alone the plant of true happiness can flourish.

— SWAMI KRIYANANDA, *The Hindu Way of Awakening*

CHAPTER TWO

An Age of Energy

... life force ... can be consciously and instantly recharged from the unlimited supply of cosmic energy.

— PARAMHANSA YOGANANDA, *Autobiography of a Yogi*

During his first lecture tours in America in the 1920s, Paramhansa Yogananda would startle his large audiences by rushing onto the stage, his long hair flying exuberantly behind him, radiating dynamic energy. *"How is everybody?"* he would shout, then lead everyone in the exuberant response, *"Awake and ready!"* Again Yogananda would shout, *"How feels everybody?"* and again join his audience with, *"Awake and ready!"*

On New Year's Eve, 1977, I visited Ananda Village, the spiritual community founded by Swami Kriyananda. It was there that I first met people who meditated and followed the path of Kriya Yoga. I saw a light in their eyes, a radiant joy in their nature, good-heartedness, and a notably high level of energy.

I had recently discovered *Autobiography of a Yogi* and was enthralled by Yogananda's accounts of yogis, saints, and miracles. Especially compelling was the chapter on Kriya Yoga, with its promise of spiritual methods that would bring people the experience of God.

I soon moved to Ananda and met Swami Kriyananda. He had become a disciple of Paramhansa Yogananda in 1948 and spent the following decades serving his Guru. Kriyananda was the first long-time yogi-saint I had ever met. Like many of those who met Yogananda in the 1920s, I was initially taken aback by what I saw.

My preconceived notions of a saint were based on a popular misconception of Jesus, as "gentle Jesus meek and mild." He is often depicted cuddling a baby sheep with a look of sentimental tenderness. In sharp contrast, Yogananda and Kriyananda were dynamos of energy. They taught with high energy and spiritual authority.

At the time when I met Kriyananda, he was composing and singing spiritual songs. He had already written several books while founding a thriving spiritual community. He was the most energetic and joyous person I had ever met.

I confess that it took months to let go of my false notions of saintliness. In time, I understood that the high states of divine joy described by Yogananda in his autobiography require an extraordinary level of energy. Successful people in every field, including the spiritual, have that same dynamic energy.

From Yogananda and Kriyananda I learned that Jesus, too, was much more than the romanticized image I had grown up with. I suspect many churchgoers mentally try to bring him down to *their* energy level, where they feel more comfortable. Yet Jesus demonstrated tremendous strength and spiritual power when he single-handedly drove the money changers out of the temple in Jerusalem.

Energy is the "missing link" between the seeker's over-identification with matter (especially the body) and identification with the pure consciousness of spirit. The key to high energy is willpower. Although strong will is often associated with ego and *self*-will, the willpower of saints and masters comes not from ego but from close alignment with *divine* will.

Yogananda once demonstrated the power of divinely attuned will in front of a large audience in Boston. He asked for volunteers to come onto the stage and test his strength. Six burly policemen jumped up and approached aggressively. Yogananda backed up against a wall and asked them to push against his stomach with their combined strength. When the six were pushing with their full force, he arched his back and sent all of them flying off the stage!

Until spiritual qualities—such as love, compassion, and joy—are empowered with divine energy, they remain more on the level of human sentiment. When they are charged with divine power, those same qualities turn into their divine counterparts. The saints are the living proof of this transformation.

Yogananda defined willpower as "desire plus energy directed toward fulfillment." Those who achieve success in any field have followed that formula, whether they know it or not. In the spiritual arena, the desire for God and inner freedom must be combined with energy—through the instrument of willpower—for the seeker to reach divine fulfillment. Yogananda often said, "The greater the will, the greater the flow of energy."

At this time, the dawning of *Dwapara Yuga*, it will take our full energy to ride the fresh waves of spiritual energy sweeping the planet. We must learn to be a *cause*, embracing the spirit of the age, rather than an *effect*, letting ourselves be swept along by the crowd.

In order to ride an ocean wave, surfers must paddle their boards at close to the speed of the wave. If they succeed, they can enjoy the thrill of riding a mighty wave to the shore. If they aren't strong enough, they may be smashed by the wave. Such is the opportunity, and the potential danger, of living in an age of increased energy.

The growing energy of these times explains why people who formerly would have reacted to life's challenges with mild irritation now become angry, even violent. On the positive side, it explains why I personally witnessed countless people in India rising above their human limitations and becoming heroes of selfless love during the pandemic of 2020–2022. Increased energy magnifies the qualities in our nature, good or bad.

To help us navigate the waters of heightened energy, it is helpful to use techniques that can help us raise our level of energy, and to control that energy.

When I began studying Yogananda's teachings, I was surprised to see that the first technique in the Kriya Yoga path was his Energization Exercises—referred to in *Autobiography of a Yogi* as "Yogoda" exercises:

Realizing that man's body is like an electric bat-
tery, I reasoned that it could be recharged with
energy through the direct agency of the human
will. As no action, slight or large, is possible
without willing, man can avail himself of his
prime mover, will, to renew his bodily tissues
without burdensome apparatus or mechanical
exercises. I therefore taught the Ranchi students
my simple "Yogoda" techniques by which the life
force, centered in man's medulla oblongata, can
be consciously and instantly recharged from the
unlimited supply of cosmic energy.

— PARAMHANSA YOGANANDA, *Autobiography of a Yogi*

Those practices not only enable us to draw on the
infinite supply of cosmic energy—they make us increasingly aware that *we are made of energy*. Awareness of that
energy dramatically hastens spiritual progress.

Yogananda's teachings on energy can help followers of all paths. Several years ago I traveled to Italy with
a group of our Ananda monks on a spiritual pilgrimage.
A Franciscan nun, showing us one of the sites associated
with St. Francis, expressed curiosity about our group. One
of our monks explained the universality of our approach
to God, and that the yoga techniques we practice are simply tools to help us reach Him. When he shared with her
the emphasis we place on sitting up with a straight spine
when praying and meditating—to allow a greater flow of
energy to rise to the brain—the Catholic nun responded
with great enthusiasm: "Yes! I'm always telling my sister

nuns, 'sit up straight when you pray!' Otherwise, they fall asleep and can't pray with attention!"

The energization exercises take advantage of the way energy naturally flows in the body. I heartily recommend them for all those who would like to experiment with conscious energy-control as an aid to achieving inner communion with God.

Daily practice of the exercises gives three main benefits: greater awareness of energy; a greater flow of energy; and greater control of energy.

Greater Awareness of Energy

Successful control of energy begins with greater *awareness* of energy. I once heard a simple aphorism from Swami Kriyananda, one that applies to many areas of life: *Awareness precedes control.*

Awareness of energy includes awareness of human emotion and feeling. When we become angry or violent, fearful or anxious, it's a sign that we have lost control of our emotional energy. Those caught up in a violent rage are often unaware of how irrationally they are behaving. Could they stop for a moment and take a deep breath, that moment of calm awareness may be all they need to become aware of just how wrongly they have been behaving.

From that calm center, it becomes possible to redirect the energy of negative emotion in a positive direction. Yoga offers us many techniques specifically designed to help us transcend our lower nature by refining, harmonizing, and redirecting our energy.

Greater Flow of Energy

During our age of increasing energy, we can also more easily *receive* divine energy and feel it flowing in and through us. This comes from sensitive awareness and an intuitive receptivity. Yogananda's energization exercises can help us not only to receive consciously from the boundless source of all energy, but to direct our energy into our bodies and our daily lives.

Greater Control of Energy

It can be a challenge to learn how to control a greater flow of energy. Not uncommonly, new Kriya Yogis perceive their lives becoming "bumpier"—a natural effect of their newly intensified energy flow. A car moving slowly over a speed bump will barely register the bump. Higher energy and higher speeds make the impact of those bumps much more dramatic. In life too, control of a higher energy ride comes naturally with experience and practice.

Energy control, or *pranayam*, is a prerequisite for attaining higher states of awareness and God-contact. Kriya Yoga and other practices that work with our inner energy are the prime techniques in our age for developing *pranayam*. To emphasize that idea, Sri Yukteswar would often sing a chant that included the words, "*pranayam* be thy religion."

From energy comes magnetism. Magnetism is so essential to spiritual success that it deserves its own chapter.

Energy generates magnetism. The stronger the flow of energy, the greater the magnetism. It is magnetism, finally, that attracts to us all that we receive in life.

— SWAMI KRIYANANDA, *Money Magnetism*

CHAPTER THREE

Change Your Magnetism

"It [*samadhi*] comes with a natural inevitability to the sincere devotee. His intense craving begins to pull at God with an irresistible force. The Lord, as the Cosmic Vision, is drawn by the seeker's magnetic ardor into his range of consciousness."

— PARAMHANSA YOGANANDA, *Autobiography of a Yogi*

The law of magnetism is the secret of success in all areas of life. A strong, positive magnetism *attracts* success, the right friends and associates, inspiration, and creativity—even spiritual progress. *Samadhi* bliss, the highest spiritual state of divine union, is not *achieved*, but in Yogananda's words, "drawn by the seeker's magnetic ardor."

Deep meditation is not an excuse to reject the world or become impractical. Immediately after Yogananda's first experience of *samadhi*, his guru handed him a broom to sweep the porch and gently chided him, "You must not get

23

overdrunk with ecstasy. Much work yet remains for you in the world."

Early in my Kriya Yoga practice I learned that there doesn't need to be a conflict between meditation and being practical. The spiritual magnetism generated by regular meditation can even attract solutions to the most mundane problems.

In 1983, Swami Kriyananda invited me to join his personal staff, soon after a crew of carpenters, plumbers, and electricians had finished a major expansion of his Crystal Hermitage home and the surrounding gardens.

My first job was to complete several projects that needed some finishing touches. I would often call expert electricians, carpenters, or plumbers for help. One unresolved problem was a strange issue with the water pipes. They were making a loud noise at a very consistent interval, over a hundred times each hour, all day long. This happened only during daylight hours, when Kriyananda was working in his office.

The most experienced plumbers could not solve the mystery. It was so annoying that Kriyananda would regularly ask me when it would be fixed. Abandoned by the experts, I saw no hope of finding a solution.

One morning as I was practicing Kriya Yoga, diligently concentrating on my practices—and not on my problems!—an uplifted feeling began to come over me. Suddenly, out of nowhere and uninvited, came inspiration—within that inspiration, came the solution to that difficult problem.

Paramhansa Yogananda wrote in his autobiography, "thoughts are universally and not individually rooted." We cannot *create* a thought, an idea, a piece of music, or a work of art. We can only tune in to—and magnetically attract to ourselves—all thoughts and ideas, both positive and negative.

In an uplifted state of consciousness, we enter the realm of genuinely inspired (not just good) ideas, creativity, solutions to problems, and divine contact. Our magnetism, transformed by meditation, draws to us the right inspiration. The opposite is also true. When we are in a negative mood, we attract negative thoughts, pessimism, and poor decisions.

Thus, Lahiri Mahasaya counseled his disciples to solve all their problems through Kriya Yoga. As I discovered, even plumbing problems can be solved through Kriya Yoga!

The science behind the electromagnet shows us that magnetism depends on a strong flow of energy. The greater the flow of energy through the wires of an electromagnet, the stronger the magnetic field.

Similarly, though on a subtler level, Kriya Yoga increases the flow of energy in our deep energy spine, which yogis call the *sushumna*. In science, as well as in the spiritual life, *the greater the flow of energy, the greater the magnetic field.* Those with a strong spiritual magnetism have a strong energy flow through their inner spine.

By increasing the flow and quality of our inner magnetism, Kriya Yoga changes our life *from the inside out.* I still recall a graphic demonstration from my early school years.

Our science teacher gave us a piece of paper, some iron filings, and a horseshoe-shaped magnet. We scattered the filings on top of the paper and held the magnet under the paper. The iron filings instantly formed into the shape of the otherwise invisible magnet field. When we moved the magnet under the paper, the iron filings also moved. If we tried to rearrange the filings with our fingers, they would always revert to the pattern of the underlying magnetism.

How often do we try to rearrange surface circumstances of our lives, only to see them revert to old, habitual patterns? Here then, is the key to success: *change your underlying magnetism, and you can change your life.*

In addition to increasing the flow of energy, we must also improve the *quality* and *direction* of that flow. Kriya Yoga gives us the ability to control the inner energy — the quality, the direction, and the intensity.

The right kind of *outward* effort to change our lives is necessary, too — meditation is not a call to inaction. People who act with energy, concentration, and an uplifted consciousness can also develop the magnetism that attracts success. Those who act in a scattered and unfocused manner, or with negativity or low energy, have only limited success. Without a change in magnetism, the iron filings of their lives will usually revert to the old patterns.

Magnetism can be strongly negative as well as positive — and can thereby attract negative thoughts, people, and failure. In our experiment with inner magnetism, if our energy flow is an always positive, upwardly directed *divine* energy, we will attract positive thoughts, inspiration, uplifting company, and success on all levels, practical as well as spiritual.

We can also change our magnetism by placing ourselves in close proximity to a stronger positive magnet.

This dimension of magnetism is discussed in chapter fourteen, "The Need for a Guide."

When spiritual magnetism begins to develop, you will find yourself less influenced by other people's negativity or anxiety. A frequent question I hear from beginning meditators is, "After my morning meditation, I feel so peaceful and calm. Then I go to the office, and suddenly I lose it! I'm much more receptive, my heart is open, and all the negativity and anger of people in the office affect me even more than before. What can I do?"

Deep meditation requires receptivity, but not passive receptivity. Passivity only weakens our magnetism. True meditation requires concentration, energy, and willpower, together with *dynamic* receptivity. Right receptivity comes naturally with time and practice. The right kind of receptivity requires the active involvement of our will.

To enhance positive receptivity when you meditate, turn the palms of your hands up, then raise your awareness and your gaze. Feel that you are offering yourself upward and receiving divine light from above. Contrast this experience with the feeling that comes with the negative moods that come with downward-directed consciousness.

You will see that as your inner spiritual magnet becomes strong, the negative influence of the world's magnetism begins to lose power. A strong magnet always influences a weaker one. Many of our difficulties in dealing with stress, fear, anxiety, desire, and attachment are simply the natural effect of the world "out there" having a stronger magnetism than the world "in here," at our spiritual center.

Sri Yukteswar affirmed, "The deeper the self-realization of a man, the more he influences the whole universe by his subtle spiritual vibrations, and the less he himself is affected by the phenomenal flux."

The spiritual power fully demonstrated in the saints is the real "superpower." It is the divine birthright of each of us. The blessing of the age of energy in which we live is that we now have the spiritual tools to develop that power.

A simple exercise for developing magnetism:

Magnetism is the secret of all success. It is the secret of all true inspiration, and of high creativity. To develop it in the best way, concentrate on the energy in the heart. Raise that energy to the point between the eyebrows, and feel that the upper part of your body is encircled by a golden light. Feel that light centered, finally, in the top of the head (the *sahasrara*, or thousand-petaled lotus). This practice will fill you with magnetism. It will fill you above all with Bliss.

Now, then, for creativity send that energy outward through the point between the eyebrows. Feel magnetism and inspiration in this outflow of energy. Direct them toward whatever task you want to work on creatively.

— SWAMI KRIYANANDA, *Ancient Keys to Attaining Success & Happiness*

CHAPTER FOUR

"*Pranayam* Be Thy Religion"

The great guru [Lahiri Mahasaya] taught his disciples to avoid theoretical discussion of the scriptures. "He only is wise who devotes himself to realizing, not reading only, the ancient revelations," he said. "Solve all your problems through meditation. Exchange unprofitable religious speculations for actual God-contact. Clear your mind of dogmatic theological debris; let in the fresh, healing waters of direct perception. Attune yourself to the active inner Guidance; the Divine Voice has the answer to every dilemma of life."

— PARAMHANSA YOGANANDA, *Autobiography of a Yogi*

A **close disciple of** Paramhansa Yogananda, Peggy Dietz, remarked to me that the Kriya Yogi is like a gardener who plants and cares for a fruit tree. The gardener doesn't

31

know precisely when the tree will bear fruit—it depends on the kind and variety of fruit, the soil, the fluctuating climate, and other factors. It may bear fruit in one year or it could be many years.

Peggy told me that the gardener's role is simple—just follow the correct practices: watering, fertilizing, pruning, and protecting the young tree from being eaten by insects or hungry animals. The gardener must also tune in to the young trees, understanding why a specific tree is not growing strong or why it is susceptible to disease or pests. Results don't come by only mechanically applying what one has learned, or "going by the book."

Peggy promised that the tree of Kriya Yoga will inevitably bear fruit in its own proper time if the yogi is conscientiously following the right practices. I could see the fruits of her own practice in the light and joy she radiated, even well into her eighties!

Theory alone—knowledge of energy and magnetism, for example—cannot free us from suffering. Regular *practice* of Kriya Yoga is needed. For those who practice in the right way, the fruit of positive change is inevitable. I have seen this proved in the lives of many hundreds of Kriya Yogis.

Success in any field requires control of the life force. Aspiring yogis and meditators must gain some degree of that control in order to overcome suffering—and even more, to be inspired at will. Does that seem impossible, to feel inspiration by willing to do so?

Yogananda, just as he was preparing to step onto a stage to give a lecture, was asked, "Is it possible for inspiration to be under the control of a person's will?" He replied, "Yes, it is. Take down this poem." That poem was later included in his book of divinely inspired prayer-poems, *Whispers from Eternity*. A reviewer singled out that particular poem as an example of the book's inspired poetry.*

The central importance of *pranayam*, control of the energy, is shown in the following chant, often sung by Sri Yukteswar. The author of the chant uses poetic license to highlight the power of life-force control:

Desire, My Great Enemy

Desire, my great enemy,
With his soldiers surrounding me; is giving me lots
    of trouble, oh, my Lord.
That enemy I will deceive, remaining in the castle of
    peace
Night and day in Thy joy, Oh, my Lord.
What will be my fate? Oh, Lord, tell me.
Pranayam be Thy religion,
Pranayam will give Thee salvation.
Pranayam is the wishing tree.
Control the little *Pranayam*, become all-pervading
    Pranayam.
You won't have to fear anything anymore.

Divine joy, fulfillment of our highest wishes, freedom from fear and desire, even salvation itself—these naturally come as the yogi develops *pranayam*. Even the beginning

---

* O Father, when I was blind I found not a door which led to Thee, but now that Thou hast opened my eyes I find doors everywhere: through the hearts of flowers, through the voice of friendship, through sweet memories of all lovely experiences. Every gust of my prayer opens a new door in the vast temple of Thy presence.

meditator discovers that techniques of *pranayam* can help control the restless thoughts that harass everyone who tries to meditate.

Because breathing techniques help us control energy, people often call the breathing exercises themselves "*pranayams*." But the *pranayam* technique of Kriya Yoga uses the physical breath mainly as a tool to gain control over the subtler, inner energies.

To repeat, *regularity* of practice is essential if we are to achieve results. Daily finger exercises on the piano gives a musicians control over the fingers, enabling them to play inspired music. Similarly, daily practice of Kriya Yoga helps the meditator develop the inner control necessary to spiritual progress. Theory alone does not make great musicians or saints.

Success in controlling our energy begins with awareness. In trying to control anything—emotions, thoughts, even the physical body in dance or athletics—awareness precedes control. To aid the meditator in developing that awareness, Yogananda preceded the teaching of Kriya Yoga with a simple technique he called *Hong-Sau*. When practiced in the inner spine, Yogananda labeled it the "baby Kriya."

With regular practice, *Hong-Sau* gives a growing awareness of the currents in the spine, an awareness that prepares the meditator for deeper practices such as Kriya. We also see the effect on our consciousness of the upward and downward currents—how downward pulling inner energy draws us into desire, attachment, and negative emotions; and how upward flowing energy awakens spiritual states such as calmness and joy.

Hong-Sau practice helps us develop the power of concentration, an important form of energy control. Control of the inner energies leads to control of the restless mind, thoughts, and feelings.

Physical stillness is an under-appreciated step to controlling the life force in meditation. Unless we can sit completely still in meditation, withdrawing the life force from the physical body (and thus controlling the life force), becomes nearly impossible. That is why Yogananda stated, "Where motion ceases, God begins."

The principles and techniques of Kriya Yoga give us a comprehensive, systematic, scientific approach to working with universal realities of body, mind, and soul. The simple task of the aspiring meditator-gardener is to follow the Guru-given guidance in establishing a daily practice.

How can we tell if we are progressing in *pranayam*?

Kriya Yogi friends have often come to me with some version of the following question, even after several years of Kriya practice: "I'm not having any experiences in meditation; am I doing something wrong?" Yet I can see for myself that over the years since they learned Kriya, they have become calmer, more compassionate and selfless, more creative and energetic, and more clear-minded. They are often beginning to look like saints!

Learn to trust that beneficial changes will come, in their own time and often in unexpected ways, when following the right practices. In later chapters, we will look at how to use *pranayam* to work directly with negative emotions such as fear and suffering. Control of life force gives us the power to lift negative, downward flowing heart-feeling into the higher octave of divine feeling: divine love and divine bliss.

"Kriya is your *Chintamani,*" Yogananda told a disciple — referring to a wish-fulfilling gem mentioned in an ancient Indian legend. The Master often spoke of the wide-ranging spiritual benefits of Kriya practice.

You will find results coming all the more quickly when you dedicate more of your daily life to the practice of meditation. Tangible results may take time because of your particular karma, or because God is testing your determination and patience. Our part, just like the gardener's, is to trust in the inevitable results. Doubt itself can delay progress; it can even pull one off the path of meditation for a lifetime or more. Learn to trust the promise that Yogananda gave, "One should hope to become a *jivan mukta** in this lifetime through the practice of Kriya Yoga."

---

* The 'fully victorious saint' is one, finally, who is what is known as 'freed while living': a *jivan mukta*. Such a person has attained *nirbikalpa samadhi*, and final victory over the supreme, indeed, the only, obstacle he ever had: his self-created burden of self-identity, self-separative, ever self-divisive from others, which forms a yawning chasm between himself and God. When a person attains this highest state at last, he will never fall again.

Control of what Yogananda used to call the "sense telephones" is essential for deep meditation. Sense control by withdrawal of the energy is the true meaning of *pranayama*: "*yama* (control) of the *prana* (energy)." *Pranayama* is a condition, not a technique. The practice of *pranayama* is to achieve energy control.

— SWAMI KRIYANANDA, *The Essence of the Bhagavad Gita*

CHAPTER FIVE

Combining Art and Science

The experience [of cosmic consciousness] can never be given through one's mere intellectual willingness or open-mindedness. Only adequate enlargement by yoga practice and devotional *bhakti* can prepare the mind to absorb the liberating shock of omnipresence.

— PARAMHANSA YOGANANDA, *Autobiography of a Yogi*

With these words, Yogananda is telling us about the need for *both* science and art in meditation. In the Bhagavad Gita, Krishna similarly says that aspiring yogis will find God when they have ". . . their minds concentrated on Me by yoga practice, *and* their hearts' feelings uplifted to Me in devotion . . ." (Bhagavad Gita, 12:6–7).

It is unfortunately common for seekers to become sidetracked by an obsession with technical proficiency in their yoga practices. The life-changing power of techniques is lost when their practice is only mechanical. Success comes with the marriage of art and science, surely a "match made in heaven."

A beautiful story of St. Francis of Assisi demonstrates this truth.

As the young Francis' reputation for sanctity began to spread, a brother monk wished to see for himself whether it was justified. As he carefully observed Francis through-out the day, he seemed to be a good and humble soul — but was he a true saint?

That night, in the room shared by all the monks, the questioning monk stayed awake, and watched Francis closely. In the middle of the night, he saw Francis rise from his bed and kneel in prayer. His simple words — "God! God! God!" repeated over and over — transported Francis into a state of divine ecstasy. His brother monk's doubts were laid to rest.

The word "God" can become no more than a platitude, a word watered down through overuse. The same word can be charged with intense devotion. If we can practice our meditation techniques with the loving fervor that Francis gave to "God! God! God!" — we, too, would be transport-ed to heavenly realms. Mechanical practice alone, on the other hand, yields very limited benefits.

If mechanical practice of techniques has limitations, so does purely devotional practice have its pitfalls. It can easily pull us downward into human, rather than divine, emotion. It is the marriage of devotion and technique that gives the best results.

Great artists and scientists have much in common with great yogi saints. Neither is only a scientist nor only an artist. The great scientist Albert Einstein once told an interviewer, "Intuition is the father of new knowledge."

Einstein's intuition, of course, was supported by the scientific understanding that was the foundation of his work. Great artists, too, combine theory, technique, and inspiration. I heard a highly skilled and inspired musician quote his music teacher's advice: "Don't let bad technique get in the way of good music."

The art side of the equation includes devotion (*bhakti* as it's called in India), right use of intuition, creativity, enthusiasm for one's practice, and working with one's feeling nature. In later chapters we'll look at these qualities, and how they can help our meditation.

Right attitude, too, is essential to the art of meditation. Yogananda said, "*Kundalini* [the inner life force] cannot be awakened by yoga techniques alone." Positive thoughts, love, and kindness are necessary in the yogi's efforts to awaken that sleeping energy and aid in its rise up the spine.

The science side of the formula includes daily practice and experience, a basic theoretical understanding, following the guidance of the Master scientist (the Guru), and proper technique.

Albert Einstein said:

> Knowledge is necessary, too. An intuitive child couldn't accomplish anything without some knowledge. There will come a point in everyone's life, however, where only intuition can make the leap ahead, without ever knowing precisely how. One can never know why, but one must accept intuition as fact.

A quality you see in the most successful scientists and artists is a high degree of enthusiasm, even passion. The enthusiasm of the aspiring meditator is more than human emotion—it is an upwardly directed, divinely inspired, calm feeling. The word "enthusiasm" derives from the Greek *en*, "within," and *theos*, "God." Lack of enthusiasm can lead to too mechanical a practice, to a drying of inspiration, and to a falling away from one's meditation practice.

Intuition is how we perceive deeper truths and God. Yogananda described intuition as *calm feeling*. Here again, we see the marriage of art and science: the calmness that comes from right practice of scientific techniques of meditation combined with divine feeling.

Intuition enables us to perceive *from the heart* rather than with the intellect. When Yogananda received his first experience of divine ecstasy, he realized it as "a point of intuitive perception in my heart"—not from the head or by thinking. God is known through intuitive feeling, not through intellectual understanding.

A cellist friend who practices Kriya plays with an inspired blend of technique and inspiration. Even though he has played for years with major orchestras, I suspect that he still practices technical exercises to maintain his proficiency. When he performs, his technique is an effortless vehicle for his inspiration.

In the same way, those who are advanced in meditation have applied themselves to learning and practicing the techniques of meditation. In their practice, even technique itself has become a devotional offering to God.

Over the years, I have seen many meditators lose themselves in the mechanics of their practice. It is better to err on the art side of the equation than on the technique side. When we have love and enthusiasm, we will have the motivation to learn and practice with right technique. We will also find it easier to maintain a lifelong practice. Our devotion will draw the grace and help of God that will, in the end, bring success.

I was taught an important lesson on how devotion can make up for imperfect technique. Once I was guiding a new Kriya Yogi, a man in his eighties. Polio as a young man had left his lungs severely compromised later in life. He had great inner energy and willpower—he had been an Olympic athlete until he contracted polio.

When I checked his Kriya technique on the morning after learning Kriya, his difficulty with breathing was so severe that it sounded nothing like Kriya. I encouraged him to do his best and to practice with devotion. Privately, I wasn't optimistic.

When I saw him a year later, I was struck by how well he looked! At that age, people seldom look better with the passing years. It was evident from his enthusiastic praise for Kriya that it was the reason for his transformation.

When he asked me to check his Kriya technique again, it was just as bad as before! I could see that he was making his best effort but simply couldn't overcome his physical limitations. I was happily surprised to see such a clear confirmation that devotion and other aspects of the Kriya art are more important than technique alone.

Try to avoid the natural tendency to over-identify with your techniques as your path or religion. The greatest artists don't self-identify as an "impressionist" or a "watercolor" artist. Similarly, the saints don't identify themselves with a particular school of technique or a specific religion. It is their followers who, often too proudly, proclaim someone as a *Hindu* saint or a *Catholic* saint. Remember the abbot of the Catholic monastery mentioned in chapter one, who greeted Yogananda simply as "Man of God"—not as a *Hindu* or *Kriya Yogi* man of God.

Put God first, practice with deep devotion, self-offering, and enthusiasm, and you will find techniques to be an extraordinary aid in your search. It bears repeating: "Do not mistake the technique for the goal." When we practice meditation techniques *with* the goal of God always in front of us, we quickly see that a perfect marriage of art and science gives life-changing results.

Science is necessary to understanding. But science is the lesser part of understanding. "Art"—that is to say, the subtle inspiration with which one applies the science—is the true essence both of understanding and of creativity. Art can never be taught, nor learned. The techniques of painting can be studied, but the subtle heart of painting must be discovered by the artist for himself. It can be neither described nor defined. If ever this art, so essential to high achievement in any field, can be acquired from anyone, it must come by a process of what may be called spiritual osmosis. It is a kind of magnetism, and must exist, well-formed, in the person who transmits it and be received by a student of already-developed sensitivity.

— SWAMI KRIYANANDA, *Art as a Hidden Message*

CHAPTER SIX

Feeling: From Human to Divine

Repeat to each of your disciples this majestic promise from the Bhagavad Gita: *"Swalpamasya dharmasya, trayata mahato bhoyat"* — "Even a little bit of the practice of this religion will save you from dire fears and colossal sufferings."

— MAHAVATAR BABAJI TO LAHIRI MAHASAYA,
Autobiography of a Yogi

Inspiration, enthusiasm, devotion, intuition — all come from the uplifted feeling of the heart. The fear and suffering mentioned in the Gita stanza above also originate in our feeling nature, along with their brethren: sorrow, grief, worry, pain, regret.

People often claim that fears and anxieties are only "in the mind." In fact, they are of the heart. What we experience in the mind, in our thoughts, is the conscious expression of what is in our heart. As Yogananda put it,

"Reason follows feeling." *Agitated feeling of the heart is the root cause of all fear and suffering.*

God, too, has been described by many sages as *feeling*—uplifted and pure feeling. Swami Kriyananda described it this way: "God is feeling, more than reason, and that feeling is bliss. We were made from that bliss." We find the same definition in the words of Adi Shankara, the reformer of Hinduism. God, he declared, is *sat chit anandam*—in Yogananda's paraphrase: "ever-existing, ever-conscious, ever-new Bliss."

In his *Yoga Sutras*, Patanjali describes *yoga* (union with the divine) as *"yogas chitta vritti nirodh"*: "yoga is the neutralization of the vortices of feeling." Yogis describe these vortices as whirlpools of energy located in the inner energy spine (*see chapter fifteen*). These *"chitta vrittis"* are vortices of feeling energy. They hold our fears and sufferings, desires and attachments—everything that binds us.

Many meditators imagine that the way to avoid suffering is to suppress or deny feeling. Some people try to kill unpleasant feeling by self-medicating with drugs or alcohol. We all know that these "cures" don't lead to lasting happiness.

Suppressing human feeling can also deaden the ability to experience pure divine feeling. Such suppression can weaken the passionate yearning required to fuel a lifetime of spiritual practice. Nor does the answer lie in indulging in our human emotions. Uncontrolled expression of emotion serves only to pull the energy further downward into deeper moods and negative feeling.

The way out is *upward*—to transmute human feeling into divine feeling. Such transmutation is part of the spiritual alchemy of practices such as Kriya Yoga. It is why the effective practice of meditation can free us from those dire fears and colossal sufferings.

I'll share a story showing how suffering can be transcended with Kriya. When I lost my wife of twenty-five years to cancer, I discovered that all of my lofty spiritual philosophy could not heal the mixed emotions of my all too human heart. We have all experienced, or will experience, the loss of a loved one. I'm sure many of you are familiar with the emotions that come up: grief, sadness, perhaps old regrets or hurts (received or given), or the wish that one could instead "live happily ever after."

I found that I couldn't philosophize my agitated feelings away. Dwelling on them also wasn't helpful, though all too easy. I knew that suppression was not the answer. Yet the downward pulling feelings were so compelling that they became a nearly constant burden—even taking over my meditations. Much as I was tempted to try to push my grief away, I understood from other experiences that the only way out was *up*: somehow to transmute that human feeling into divine feeling.

Daily I began, during Kriya practice and at other times, offering that human feeling of grief—and its positive component of human love—from my heart to God. Results didn't come instantly. Even now I continue to work on the process.

In the end, persistence in working *with* the feeling, rather than pushing it aside, gave results that far exceeded my expectations. Rather than the grief simply "going away" or just "moving on"—as some well-meaning friends told me would eventually happen—that grief became transmuted into a divine love and a much purer soul connection. It has become one of the greatest gifts of my life.

Yogananda described this alchemy in a chant: "Touch me but once and I will change, all my clay into Thy gold."

He taught that God has eight aspects by which we can experience Him: peace, calmness, sound, light, love, bliss, power, and wisdom. Especially important are the two aspects closest to our origin in God: divine love and divine bliss. These are also the two which are predominantly feeling-based.

Devotion, or love for God, is the essential ingredient in the art and the science of the spiritual life. Sri Yukteswar — a saint of pure wisdom, more than of devotion — wrote that we "cannot take one step on the spiritual path without the natural love of the heart."

Have you ever wondered *why* we've been given this natural love of the heart? Human feeling can be the *cause* of so much suffering! While human feeling does have its fulfillments — in friendship, romantic love, the love between parents and their children — these are transitory and imperfect. Why, then, are we given human parents, children, siblings, friends, and lovers?

Many spiritual people conclude that human relation-ships are *only* a stumbling block on the path to freedom. I think, rather, that God gave us these relationships as a breadcrumb trail to lead us back home. He gave us human feeling and human love to show us *how* to love, imperfect-ly at first — and from humble, human beginnings, to learn the much higher divine love.

So crucial is learning to love others that Yogananda declared, "Don't imagine that God will come to you if you behave unkindly to others. Until you know how to win human love, you will never win God's love."

Isn't there an innate understanding that the heart is our true center of awareness? When you point to yourself and say, "me," or "that's mine," do you point to your head or your chest?

It is in the heart, too, that we hold our past hurts and traumas—the many sufferings "which are inherent in the unceasing cycles of death and rebirth," as Krishna says in the Bhagavad Gita. Every suffering can be transmuted into something much higher if we can only learn how. Kriya Yoga shows us *how*.

Years ago, someone I had been trying to help deliberately hurt me. I knew the value of forgiveness—again, as a lofty philosophy—but I couldn't find it within myself to forgive that person.

Every year, Ananda follows a tradition begun by Yogananda of holding an eight-hour group meditation just before Christmas. At the end of one such all-day meditation, with my heart's feelings divinely uplifted, the person I had struggled to forgive came into my mind. Suddenly, overwhelmingly, I felt only deep unconditional love. I could easily see past my own hurt and into the hurts that caused the unkind behavior. There was no longer any need to *try* to forgive. My human feeling of hurt was transmuted into the much higher feeling of divine love and compassion.

Isn't this transmuted feeling what Christ expressed on the cross? In the midst of his agony, he called out on behalf of his torturers, "Forgive them, Father, they know not what they do" (Luke 23:34). Do you think he forgave because he suddenly remembered his own teaching and thought, "oh, I'd better forgive these people, or I'll regret it"? Or did he forgive because divine love flows naturally through an uplifted heart?

We've talked about suffering. Let's look now at the "dire fears" of Krishna's admonition. Fear may well be the most fundamental human emotion. It's possible that without fear, the human race would have perished.

But is fear the best way to respond to all of the threats and challenges that we face in modern times? Aren't most of our fears irrational and even self-defeating? Scientists have learned that the "fight or flight" response triggered by fear comes from a lower part of the brain — a part well designed for survival in more primitive humans and animals. But in modern times, the fight or flight response is more often a cause, even a multiplier, of anxiety and stress.

As yogis we can learn to transmute the feeling of fear into a high level of divine feeling. I'll share an experience of using the Kriya Yoga teachings to do so. I've seen many others do the same. I tell these stories not because I've mastered these things. If I had, I probably wouldn't have faced so many challenges in the first place! My purpose is simply to show that anyone can use these practices to overcome fear and suffering.

Years ago, I began to experience extreme chronic pain in the nerves of my face. The pain caused severe weakness, dizziness, and nausea — there were many days when I could hardly stand up.

Neurologists told me that the condition was unlikely to go away, and that it would probably get worse over the course of my life. Not exactly comforting news! Nonetheless, I never gave up looking for a solution.

There were periods when I was utterly incapable of functioning. At the worst times, there arose the natural fear: "What if I have this condition for the rest of my life? Can I handle this pain? How will I support myself and function in the world? What a burden I will be to others!"

After months of failing to find a solution, there was a night when I reached a point of despair. In my despair, I surrendered — not giving up, but surrendering to God. I have long followed Swami Kriyananda's practice of not praying for myself. Instead, I offered myself at the feet of God in the form of the Divine Mother. I asked nothing *for* myself from God, but only to *give* myself completely. In this way, I was able to give my unconditional love to the Divine Mother, and as Her child, to scold Her lightheartedly for treating Her child in such a miserable way!

In that moment of self-forgetfulness, of complete devotional self-offering, I was overwhelmed by the tremendous feeling of divine joy. The physical pain and the fear were still there, but they had receded far into the background as the much more powerful feeling of Her grace came to the fore. I believe that moment was the beginning of my healing, on both physical and emotional levels.

The same challenge still visits me every few years. Now, when it comes, I see it as a reminder to go deeper within — into the ultimate antidote for fear, which is divine love. I hope you will learn, as I have, to have deep gratitude for the uninvited pains and sufferings that come in life. Without them, I would not have experienced their higher, divine counterparts. It isn't always easy, but I have learned to see all tests as divine gifts.

The relationship between fear and its opposite, divine love, is demonstrated by a character in the Indian epic, the *Mahabharata*, of which the Bhagavad Gita is one part. Paramhansa Yogananda said that the characters in the Mahabharata represent our psychological traits and how they influence our lives.

Certain characters in the *Mahabharata*, he explained, represent the different *chakras* or spinal energy centers. The five *Pandava* brothers, heroes of the story, represent the five chakras leading up to and including the throat center. The heart center is represented by the impetuous Bhima, the largest and strongest of the brothers. He was usually chosen to defeat the strongest enemies. Bhima is fearless — his strength and courage are limitless.

We don't usually think of courage and strength as coming from divine love, yet we say of brave warriors or athletes, "They have a lot of heart."

When Bhima's great heart energy runs out of control, he is the most emotional of the brothers and often finds himself in trouble. But when that same energy is directed upward, it manifests as tremendous physical strength, power, selflessness, and courage.

Bhima's eldest brother Yudhishthira is the calm one, who often tames Bhima's angry outbursts. Yudhishthira represents the throat chakra, the seat of calmness in the astral spine. This same heart energy, directed upward as calm divine feeling, is powerfully magnetic. The Indian cartoon character, Choto Bhim — "little child Bhima" — is portrayed as highly magnetic and lovable, even as a small child able to defeat demons.

Such is the magnetism of divine love—the "divine magnetic ardor" of which Yogananda lovingly speaks. Divine love is a magnetism that comes naturally as the result of upward-flowing love for God.

The main—indeed, the only important thing on the spiritual path is to calm the emotions. Calm feeling is love, which unites the soul with God. Restless or agitated feelings, on the other hand—our emotions—disrupt our vision and prevent us from achieving full acceptance that in our true reality we are manifestations of the eternal stillness of God.

— SWAMI KRIYANANDA, *Demystifying Patanjali*

CHAPTER SEVEN

The Fire of Devotion

The yogi offers his labyrinthine human longings to a monotheistic bonfire dedicated to the unparalleled God. This is indeed the true yogic fire ceremony, in which all past and present desires are fuel consumed by love divine.

— PARAMHANSA YOGANANDA, *Autobiography of a Yogi*

Successful people have a fiery passion for their interest, whether it is science, business, or the arts—this is notably true of the saints. When Yogananda was a small boy, simply hearing someone speak the name of God would awaken tears of longing.

Many people begin the spiritual path with great fervor, often experiencing quick results. The early stages of the divine quest can feel like a honeymoon—the devotee is filled with the fresh enthusiasm of a wonderful beginning, and convinced that the intensity of the heart's fiery feelings will never die. But there comes a time when

God tests our love, sending us karmic challenges of restlessness, doubt, and dry periods — much like in human relationships.

In my first years at Ananda, many of us would regularly read *Autobiography of a Yogi* and the lives of the saints to keep that love alive. Inspired company too is important. That brought me through a very long dry spell.

Living in the first Ananda monastery, I was surrounded by brother monks who were a constant source of inspiration. We held group meditations, morning and evening, and a five-hour meditation on Saturday morning. Despite the ideal environment, I hit a long dry patch. The early joys and seemingly effortless progress suddenly vanished. The test lasted for a surprisingly long time.

I continued to show up for group meditations, but I couldn't help feeling that I was wasting my time! I wasn't experiencing results, and with wry humor, I thought that I might as well bring a newspaper, because I could at least be learning something while I sat.

One day I had a change of attitude — inspired I'm sure by lessons learned from the lives of the saints and by the inspiring company I was keeping. I stopped my mental grumbling — "What am I *getting* out of this?" — and decided that even though I didn't seem to be *receiving* anything from God, I could at least *give* myself to Him. I could give Him my thoughts, attention, and the meager bit of love I felt, and perhaps my prayers for other people whose sufferings were worse than my own.

That decision began a complete turnaround — from dryness and boredom, to a practice that brought me a lasting, far more mature kind of inspiration. It brought home to me very strongly a truth that Krishna expresses in the Bhagavad Gita and that Swami Kriyananda beautifully explained:

> A single spark may start a forest fire. The smallest step toward God can be a beginning in the process of soul-awakening. The Bhagavad Gita says, "To him who offers Me even a flower or a leaf with devotion, I Myself come and receive his offering." The smallest expression of pure love can be the spark that ignites a fire of devotion which ultimately consumes the forest of our desires and leaves our consciousness free to soar untrammeled in infinite skies.
>
> — SWAMI KRIYANANDA, *The Promise of Immortality*

One of the greatest secrets for keeping the flame of devotion alive is to learn to *give* ourselves to God, even when all we have to offer are the smallest flowers or leaves of a very restless heart. We find then that it truly is "more blessed to give than to receive."—"Blessed," in the sense of "blissful."

In his autobiography, *The New Path: My Life with Paramhansa Yogananda*, Swami Kriyananda includes a chapter on Kriya Yoga that starts with Jesus's words: "Blessed are the pure in heart, for they shall see God" (Matthew, 5:8). Purity of heart, he explains, is the capacity to love God with *all* one's heart, soul, mind, and strength.

Devotion, power, and inner strength—these aren't qualities we often think of together. Worldly people view devotion as nothing more than a sweet sentiment. Others associate it with excessively emotional spiritual practices—the followers of some Christian sects roll on the floor, "inspired" by what Yogananda called the "Unholy Ghost of emotion." In East and West, singing, chanting, and dancing can descend from pure devotion to superficial emotional agitation.

Outward practices can help us *start* to awaken the heart's feelings, but the *power* of devotion comes when that energy is calm, interiorized, and directed intensely upwards. When we can offer our heart's longing into the infinite power of divine love, we set in motion a chain reaction that lifts us into divine freedom. This is the fruit of cooperating with divine grace, a key spiritual practice we will discuss in the next chapter.

A shining example of the power of divine love is seen in the life of the great Bengali saint, Ananda Moyi Ma. Her love for God brought her such bliss that one disciple was inspired to give her the name Ananda Moyi Ma—"Bliss-permeated Mother." Swami Kriyananda once visited her in India, describing the way she walked as though marching like an army general—powered not by human will but by the Divine.

A Christian saint of the nineteenth century in France, St. Jean Vianney (also known as the Curé d' Ars), said of God's love, "Did we but know how our Lord loves us, we should die of joy!" Again we see one of God's saints associating divine love with its related feeling-fruit: divine bliss.

Even long time devotees of God can fail to distinguish between human emotion and true devotion. As we proceed on our journey, we find that it is not essential to define what we are feeling, but to keep the flow of that feeling burning and moving in the right direction.

Emotion is what we feel when the heart's energy is agitated or moving downward and outward. That includes all positive and negative human emotions — from human love and anger to desire and attachment, fear and suffering. Devotion comes when that feeling energy is directed calmly inward and upward toward God. Our task is to begin where we are now, and work to awaken and redirect our feeling energy.

Devotional chanting is one excellent way to awaken and offer our feelings to God. Paramhansa Yogananda taught an approach to chanting very different from what is commonly practiced in India or America.

During my first visit to Ananda Village, I wandered into the temple before the beginning of the Sunday service, drawn by singing unlike anything I had ever heard. I was moved to tears, although I couldn't understand why. Later, I realized that it was the first time I had heard songs sung from the heart and offered *to* God. The hymns that I'd grown up with were songs *about* God. They didn't have the direct, intimate relationship with God that I felt in the simple, heartfelt songs I heard that day.

I heard something else that was different that day. Yogananda taught that when chanting, it helps to start by singing more loudly, in order to awaken the heart's feelings — even to sing with outward emotion. Then we can chant more softly and with an increasingly inward feeling. Then mentally only, still with deep feeling. Finally, we can take the pure feeling of the chant into silent meditation. Try to practice in a directional flow: from a more outward *human* feeling-flow toward an inwardly and upwardly directed *divine* feeling-flow.

We don't want to get stuck in emotional chanting, which Yogananda called "straw fire" devotion. Yet we often need that first emotional flame to light the fire of devotion. Having lived in cold climates most of my life, I've spent many winters using a wood stove for heat. I've seen the need for first lighting newspaper or straw to ignite the long, slow burning wood that produces lasting warmth.

So it is with the journey of the heart—we can begin with the quick, hot flame of emotional longing for God, then make the fire gradually strong, calm, and steady—a fire that can last an entire lifetime.

The Sanskrit term *bhakti* is generally translated as "devotion." But "devotion" implies distance between the devotee and God—a relationship of "I" loving "Thou," each in a separate place. *Bhakti*'s true meaning is all encompassing—mutual participation, a love that devotee and God feel together, as one.

We see this active participation *in* divine love in stories about Krishna. Even as a child cowherd, Krishna was seen as a divine incarnation by those with soul perception, many of whom were woman cowherds, or *gopis*.

Accounts of the *gopis* dancing with Krishna throughout the night have been misinterpreted by scholars as merely human love, bringing the meaning down to their own level of understanding. But the real meaning is much deeper. The stories portray a relationship with God far more intimate and participatory than is found in many religions, especially in the West.

When we pray or meditate, it is helpful to begin by praying *to* God or meditating *on* God. As we go deeper, however, we find it more fulfilling to pray *in* God and meditate *in* God. Therein lies the divine union meant by the word *yoga*.

Until we can transmute human feeling into divine feeling, there will always be the danger of love slipping back into the timeworn groove that leads down and out into human emotions and desires. Once, after a long seclusion in the Himalayas, Swami Kriyananda was feeling an overwhelming love for God. Soon after, he visited Ananda Moyi Ma. Sensing what he was experiencing, she cautioned him, "Intense feeling in the heart can flow downward in the spine as well as upward."

Yoga offers us effective ways to calm the emotions and direct them towards God. The spiritual path really is that simple! It is also very short — as a friend of mine remarked, it is only thirty inches long! — from the base of the spine, to the spiritual eye at the point between the eyebrows.

The yogi must "make love to God" with technique *and* devotion. Techniques such as Kriya show us how to concentrate one-pointedly and direct calm, devotional feeling upwards. To be truly effective, Kriya must be practiced with love and a sense of sacred self-offering. Only then will it become more than a breathing technique.

I was surprised once to read Swami Kriyananda explain that the "heart's energy must, therefore, be directed deliberately — even, to some extent, austerely — upward to God."

As strange as it sounds to offer divine love "austerely," that highest love does have an impersonal dimension. It is not the "puppy love" of youngsters first falling in love, with eyes only for each other. It is the expansion of personal love to include all souls, even all creation.

Tests, too, help us develop a more mature and long-lasting love for God. We must all wonder at times why God chooses to test our love. Surely He isn't a strict taskmaster who will not pass us unless we earn high marks. We are tested because *we* need to realize and develop a love that is completely unconditional. As Kriyananda says in a song about Rama and Sita: "Only tested love is blessed."

Watch your life experiences—over time I think you will find, as I have, that every test met and overcome deepens our ability to love more purely and selflessly.

What if we aren't feeling devotion? Yogananda urged us to pray to the Divine Mother *for* devotion—that is the one thing God most wants to give us. An Indian friend of mine once asked Swami Kriyananda, "What should we most ask for from God, *bhakti* (devotion) or *mukti* (liberation)?"

With tears in his eyes, he replied by singing, in Bengali, a song written by Yogananda—*Divine Mother's Song to the Devotee*. Here is the English translation:

> Oh devotee, I can give thee salvation,
>> but not My love and devotion;
>>> for when I give those away, I give Myself away.
> Ask of Me salvation, but not My love and devotion;
>> for when I give those away, I become poor, walk-
>>> ing on your heart's wave.

The song's real meaning, hidden behind Her teasing hint of the opposite, is that Divine Mother *wants to give us devotion more than anything*, more even than salvation. When She gives Her love and devotion, She has nothing of value left to give. In this way, She is telling us that Her love and devotion *alone* are worth praying for. Whether we are in this world or a higher one, when we have that Love, we have everything we've ever wanted. We are free in God, untouched by all lower desires and attachments.

The more we can develop pure love of the heart, the more we enter into the flow of divine grace. Everything that we are seeking comes, in the end, by God's grace. Our part is to cooperate with that grace, to offer ourselves with devotion into the flow of grace. Understanding that God knows better than we do what we need, we should pray most of all for devotion. It will carry us most quickly to the divine goal.

. . . *Chitta* is more than an *aspect* of consciousness: It *is* consciousness. In man, *chitta* is far more than the reactive feelings in his heart: It is deep, intuitive feeling, which defines the very consciousness of self. In divine consciousness, *chitta* becomes cosmic feeling: not that of the ego, but of the divine Self: Absolute Bliss.

— SWAMI KRIYANANDA, *The Essence of the Bhagavad Gita*

CHAPTER EIGHT

Cooperating with Grace

Ordinary love is selfish, darkly rooted in desires and satisfactions. Divine love is without condition, without boundary, without change. The flux of the human heart is gone forever at the transfixing touch of pure love.

— SWAMI SRI YUKTESWAR, QUOTED IN *Autobiography of a Yogi*

Divine grace is like the strong current in the middle of a swiftly flowing river. Most people are trying to make progress in life by using only their limited personal strength.

To enter the central current of a river, much effort is needed simply to reach the banks of the river. Then comes the hard slogging through the mud to enter the river itself. Great will and energy are needed to fight through the currents close to the shore. When we finally reach the center of the river, the strong current, added to our strength, carries us effortlessly to the sea.

In the same way, right effort on the spiritual path, combining technique and devotion, brings us to the point where our "efforts end in ease," as Yogananda said, and we are carried home on powerful currents of divine grace.

Too many worshipers believe that divine grace is bestowed only as a gift from God—that we cannot earn it through good works or actions. There is truth to this. God is not a merchant, trading His grace for our meager gifts. But it's an all too common mistake to think of the mysterious workings of grace as an excuse for passivity.

The saints are people of great willpower and energy. They understand that we must *cooperate with grace*. That kind of cooperation is not passive; it requires the full commitment of our energy.

Paramhansa Yogananda said that success on the path comes twenty-five percent by our own effort, twenty-five percent through the guru's effort on our behalf, and fifty percent by God's grace. "Don't forget, however," he warned, "that the twenty-five percent that is your part represents one hundred percent of your own effort and sincerity!"

During a pilgrimage in India, I experienced this truth firsthand. Early one morning, just outside the town of Rishikesh, I walked with a friend to an isolated bank of the Ganges River to meditate.

There is a tradition in India that bathing in the Ganges washes away our sins. After meditating, I waded into the river to receive its blessing. Suddenly I found myself stuck in quicksand, unable to lift either of my legs out of the cement-like substance. Because I had been mired in quicksand many years earlier, I was familiar with its ways and not very alarmed. At the same time, I knew there was no way I could free myself without help.

I was in the quicksand up to my thighs, with solid ground under my feet. The fortunately calm river was at the level of my chest. I was as stuck as I've ever been in my life. Luckily, my friend was standing on solid ground. It was relatively easy to guide him to a safe place in the river where he could reach out and pull me free.

If I had only passively held out my hand, I would still be stuck. If I had tried to free myself only with my own strength, foolishly believing I should assert my independence of any need for help, I would still be stuck. Most important, it required *actively* cooperating with my friend who saved me.

There is a saying, "When we lift one hand up to God, He lowers two hands to pick us up." Grace does not come to those who wait passively for it, or who pray for it with little energy. When I called out and reached out with my full energy, God reached out through the hands of my friend.

Only the right effort can help us enter the full flood of divine grace. Right effort begins with devotion—with an intensity that includes sincerity, energy, and one-pointed purpose. Such intensity helps us develop the discipline to maintain a strong spiritual practice—day after day, year after year.

Yogananda called that kind of unceasing effort "the discipline that brings His grace." We may not think of discipline as a way to attract grace, until we understand that it arises out of our increasing love for God. The power of devotion gives *active expression* to that love. It is the kind of love that motivates a mother to shake heaven and earth to find a cure for her sick child.

Yogananda told a story showing how such devotion draws God's grace:

> A certain man was dying of diabetes. The doctors had given him only three months to live. He decided, "If all that I have left to me is three months, let me spend them in seeking God."
>
> Gradually he disciplined himself to sit in meditation for longer and longer periods every day. And all the while he kept praying, "Lord, come into this broken temple."
>
> Three months passed, and he was still alive. A year passed. Continuing his intense prayer, he gradually increased his time of meditation to eighteen hours a day.
>
> Two more years passed.
>
> After three years, suddenly a great light filled his being. He was caught up in ecstasy. On returning from that divine state, he found that his body had been healed.
>
> "Lord," he prayed, "I didn't ask for a healing. All I asked was that You come to me."
>
> And the voice of the Lord answered, "Where My light is, there no darkness can dwell."
>
> The saint then wrote with his finger on the sand, "And on this day the Lord came into my broken temple and made it whole!"

The tools of yoga help us cooperate with divine grace, to the extent that we practice with humility, devotion, and self-offering. Only by actively cooperating with grace can we reach the final stage of divine freedom. Referring to the Kriya technique, Swami Kriyananda said, ". . . every Kriya should be an act of devotional self-offering. For everything comes, in the end, by God's grace."

Receptivity is also essential to grace. God's grace is always shining, like the bright sun on the side of a building. God loves His children equally. He loves the saint as much as he loves the sinner. If we keep the curtain of our heart closed, the sunlight of His love cannot penetrate, and we won't receive what He wants to give us. When our heart is open, the light of His grace and love can enter and change us. When we close our hearts with restlessness, desire, and attachment, we prevent the ever-present rays of His grace from entering.

We must also express divine qualities in our daily lives to cooperate completely with grace. Many people attend church or temple regularly, or have a regular meditation practice, but seem to think that their practices will compensate for unkind, uncharitable, or judgmental behavior. Our thoughts and actions can separate us from the flow of grace, as surely as they can put us in tune with it.

Those who have been changed by grace find it natural, even necessary, to share it with others. If our spiritual practices aren't inspiring us with increasing generosity and kindness, we may need to rethink what we're doing. Spiritual growth will always find expression in expansive attitudes and behavior. Our ultimate perfection may be a long way off, but the *direction* of our growth is an accurate gauge of the effectiveness of our practice.

What are some signs of grace? A growing kindness towards others. Generosity of spirit. More and more self-lessness and giving to others. Compassion and empathy. These all are active expressions of love. Grace also lifts our consciousness into calmness, into a growing awareness of the presence of God, and gives us the desire for wholesome activities. The uplifting power of grace is felt not as a giddy emotional "high," but as a quiet, sure, inward joy.

In guiding Kriya Yogis over the years, I've had the joy of seeing many fruits of the grace that come with Kriya practice. An Indian woman told me that her husband was the first in the family to take up a strong meditation practice. At first, she was alarmed, fearing that he would renounce the world and go off to meditate in a cave in the Himalayas, abandoning her and the children.

Indeed, her husband changed, but not in the way she feared. With great joy, she told me how he was much less prone to anger and had become a kinder and more understanding husband and father. I was charmed by her husband's calm smile as he stood beside her and heard her talk about his transformation. He was in the military and not at all a passive person. After witnessing the changes in him, his wife joined him in practicing Kriya.

I have seen and heard of many miraculous transformations, in myself and in those I am closest to. The fruits of grace come inevitably when the gardener-yogi lovingly waters the tree of regular meditation practice.

Grace, and the love behind it, is the most powerful magnet in the universe. When we offer our heart up to God and cooperate with His grace, a powerful magnet draws us inexorably upward. The soul has a natural buoyancy that *wants* to rise. Thus, cooperating with grace means cooperating with our own higher soul-nature.

The One who created us has waited a very long time for us to offer ourselves back into Him. God *wants* to draw us into His love. That is why good works or gifts alone cannot buy His grace. God already *is* those gifts—He already has everything—except for one thing: our freely given love. God is waiting for us to give that ultimate offering of our own self.

I understand, now, that every Kriya should be an act of devotional self-offering. For everything comes, in the end, by God's grace. Grace is like sunlight on the side of a building. If the curtains of one room are kept closed, grace will not be able to enter there. Human effort is necessary, but that effort must be in cooperation with God's will. Such effort is indeed necessary, as a means of removing any and every ego-created obstacle to the sunlight of God's grace. Beyond that point, however, self-effort will only strengthen the ego. This is where yoga comes in, but it must be performed with an attitude of aligning one's egoic will with God's will; it must not strengthen the ego.

— SWAMI KRIYANANDA

CHAPTER NINE

Control the Reactive Process

The advanced yogi, withholding all his mind, will, and feeling from false identification with bodily desires, uniting his mind with superconscious forces in the spinal shrines, thus lives in this world as God hath planned, not impelled by impulses from the past nor by new witlessnesses of fresh human motivations. Such a yogi receives fulfillment of his Supreme Desire, safe in the final haven of inexhaustibly blissful Spirit.

— PARAMHANSA YOGANANDA, *Autobiography of a Yogi*

imagine that Yogananda's lighthearted words, "new witlessnesses of fresh human motivations" will be humorously familiar to most of us. To win our daily struggle with wrong motivations, we must understand what he called the *reactive process*, described here by Swami Kriyananda:

75

The upward and downward currents in *iḍa* and *pingala* [two of the spinal channels] relate directly to the waves of our own reactive process—the likes and dislikes which form the basis of our delusion. By concentrating on these inner currents rather than on the specific outward objects of our likes and dislikes, we can gradually bring our entire reactive process under control, ultimately neutralizing it.

— SWAMI KRIYANANDA, *The Art and Science of Raja Yoga*

Our *reactions* to external events—influenced by our likes and dislikes—are the true cause of suffering. Many minds rebel at that idea. The outer dramas of life are so compelling! The mind so easily thinks that what happens *to* us is the real problem, and that all we need to do is fix or avoid outer events.

The enlightened yogi, instead, says to himself, "no, you only think it's happening out there. The reality is that it's all happening in here, in your reaction to events and desires."

To help us understand the reactive process, let's imagine some dramatic event. After purchasing many lottery tickets over the years, we find that we've won. Suddenly, we're a millionaire!

Imagine your reaction—the excited intake of breath, corresponding to a rising energy in the spine as you absorb the news. You feel lighter, happier, energized. After a moment to collect yourself, you double-check the numbers, and—oops!—you realize that you were looking at last week's numbers! Suddenly you've lost your million-dollar bonanza! You let out a long, slow sigh, as your energy falls.

Outwardly nothing has changed—the only difference is your reaction and the inner flow of energy. You can also see how closely your physical breath is related to your mood swings.

The intimate connection between breath, energy, and feeling explains why many yoga techniques, including Kriya, make use of the physical breath to help us gain control of our emotions and inner energy.

The yogis teach that the very *cause* of elation and sorrow is the energy in the spine, and that moods are not caused by anything outside of our own self. Kriya Yoga helps us to become aware that the real source of joy or suffering is within. Kriya gives us the means to control that inner energy, and to control the reactive process.

One who has fully gained that control is free from all suffering, untouched by outward events and their influence. In Yogananda's words, that yogi remains ever "safe in the final haven of inexhaustibly blissful Spirit."

You may ask, "what about us mortals who don't have such superhuman control?" Here is the story of one such mortal who overcame a strong fear of death before the time of actual passing.

My wife was a Kriya Yogi for the last thirty-five years of her life. She could not let go of an irrational—for a yogi—fear of death. For ten of those years she fought a courageous battle with breast cancer. After the cancer was in remission, she began feeling symptoms of something not right in her brain. Her clear intuition told her that the cancer had returned and spread to the brain. Within days, extreme dizziness and vision problems took away her ability to stand by herself.

She was completely at peace — even beyond peace, hers was a state of joyful freedom. When I made an appointment for an MRI scan on her brain, she laughed, "If I don't have brain tumors, I'll eat my socks!"

As I wheeled her through the hospital corridor for the brain scan, she remained calm and quiet. Meanwhile I was falling prey to the extremes of my emotional reactive process. She sensed my turmoil. A true yogi, instead of comforting me emotionally, she quietly said , "Detach yourself. Control the reactive process. Live the teachings."

The MRI indeed showed many tumors in her brain. The doctor wouldn't say how many, only that she had no more than a few weeks to live. Maria spent those last few weeks in an elevated state of calm joy. Among her last words to me, spoken with inexpressible joy, were, "Don't worry, I'm free."

Her practice of Kriya, in cooperation with divine grace, had freed her of any negative reactive fear towards death. Lest you think hers is a rare story, I highly recommend the book, *Transitioning in Grace* by Ananda author Nalini Graeber. Nalini tells Maria's story, along with those of many more Kriya Yogis who made similarly joyful final passages through the last stage of life.

Inner freedom amidst the seemingly endless emotional ups and downs of life is the final proof of the practical science of Kriya. It gives a freedom that can be attained by all who follow it sincerely, as Yogananda so clearly promised:

> Practice Kriya night and day. It is the greatest key
> to salvation. Other people go by books and outer
> disciplines, but it will take them incarnations to
> reach God that way. Kriya is the greatest way of
> destroying temptation. Once you feel the inner
> joy it bestows, no evil will be able to touch you.

Control of the reactive process brings together all of the parts of the art and science of Kriya Yoga that we've discussed. This control is one of the great fruits of *pranayama*. It calms the agitated feelings that hide our true soul nature. It gives us the ability to offer ourselves completely to God, holding nothing back. It is a direct way of cooperating with grace. It frees us from dire fears and sufferings. It gives us freedom from karma and control of our own destiny.

That inner freedom is a great game-changer on the spiritual path. Gradually, and then completely, one is unaffected by the ups and downs imposed by karma and a fickle world. Under all circumstances we can feel the same calm joy — the fruit not of a heart deadened to grief and suffering, but of sensitive attunement to the divine joy within.

Kriya Yoga transforms everyone into the highest versions of themselves, as divine human beings, as parents, teachers, artists, scientists, and friends. You will find yourself becoming a cause for change in your own life and in the lives of others — proactive rather than reactive.

Control of the reactive process gives us freedom from the wheel of karma and reincarnation. When we no longer react to events in life with "new witlessnesses" and wrong choices, we no longer create the manifold wrong karmas that keep us bound in suffering, life after life.

Kriya is based on certain universally known (because experienced) facts of human nature. Of course, it takes one far beyond common experience, but its fundamentals can be observed by anybody.

The Kriya science begins with the physical symptoms accompanying emotional reaction. In this reactive process, when one is delighted by, let us say, a sudden and unexpected gift, he tends instinctively to take a quick, sharp breath. When, on the contrary, one meets with a sudden setback, the automatic tendency of people is to blow the breath out. Exultation is accompanied by inhalation, followed perhaps, by a glad cry. Gloom or disappointment is accompanied by a heavy sigh.

If you think about it, you will see that your actual reality lies not in outer things, but in your inner reaction to them. It is because watching a beautiful sunset makes you inwardly happy that you continue watching it. If that same sunset makes any impact at all on a turtle, it may be only to waken the idle question in its mind as to whether it is something good to eat. One finds difficulty in even imagining a turtle gazing at a sunset in rapt wonder. To the turtle, the sunset must hardly even exist. What makes that sunset real for human beings is the fact that they feel enough stimulated by it to react to it.

— SWAMI KRIYANANDA, *Paramhansa Yogananda:*
A Biography

CHAPTER TEN

Karma, Kriya, and Action

The science of *Kriya Yoga*, mentioned so often in these pages, became widely known in modern India through the instrumentality of Lahiri Mahasaya, my guru's guru. The Sanskrit root of *Kriya* is *kri*, to do, to act and react; the same root is found in the word *karma*, the natural principle of cause and effect. *Kriya Yoga* is thus "union (yoga) with the Infinite through a certain action or rite." A yogi who faithfully follows its technique is gradually freed from karma or the universal chain of causation.

— PARAMHANSA YOGANANDA, *Autobiography of a Yogi*

The word *kriya* comes from the same Sanskrit root as the word karma, but with a slightly different connotation. *Kriya* implies pure or selfless action, including religious rites done to please God. Actions performed selflessly, without expectation of personal reward, are liberating rather than binding. The Bhagavad Gita is full of insights on how to use right action to free us from bondage. *Karma yoga*, or selfless service, is one form of right action.

When we act out of ignorance, or with selfish motives, we set in motion a cycle of cause and effect — an expression of the law of karma.

The Kriya Yoga technique, performed correctly, is a pure selfless action, an inward religious rite. Kriya's effectiveness comes when practiced as an act of devotional giving, rather than for personal gain.

There was a disciple of Yogananda who practiced Kriya many hours a day, once meditating for forty hours straight. He acted with the goal of being spiritually rewarded for his efforts. Soon after, he left the guru, discouraged by his lack of progress.

Yogananda commented:

> He will never find God that way! He is like a merchant who says, "Lord, I have given you so many Kriyas; now You have to keep Your side of the bargain and give me so much realization." God never responds to such mercenary devotion! He accepts nothing less from us than our unconditional love.

Just as in karma yoga there is no thought of personal gain, so in meditation the best results come when we meditate only to please God. Whether you follow Kriya or another meditation path, try to practice without the thought of what you will be receiving. Instead, as Krishna advises in the *Bhagavad Gita*, give even the fruits of your practice to God.

The practice of Kriya is similar to the *puja* ceremony performed in India. *Puja* includes offerings made to God at the altar—the offerings are seen as becoming holy. Food that is offered becomes *prasad*, or sacred food. The deeper meaning of *puja* is that anything offered with love into the light of God is transformed by that light and made holy. Kriya practice is an inner *puja* ceremony, where we offer ourselves into the grace of God, who lovingly transforms the human clay of our delusion into the gold of divine freedom.

Outward action, too, when performed with selfless devotion, sanctifies the giver. Swami Kriyananda told the story of a woman who requested a past-life reading from Edgar Cayce, a famous American psychic. The woman told Cayce that she was employed as a model, and that she was in great demand by photographers who wanted to photograph her unusually beautiful hands. Edgar Cayce told her that in a past life she had been a nun and had used her hands to scrub the convent floors with great devotion. Because of the purity of her devotional offering, her hands had been blessed.

Kriya Yogis find that performing the inner action of Kriya as an act of devotional giving begins to transform their outward actions. For this reason they find it increasingly natural to give themselves more easily in service to God and in kindness toward others.

As we grow in performing all action selflessly, action itself helps us grow in freedom. Thus we see that Kriya Yoga is more than a practice limited to the meditation room—it becomes a way of life.

What about past actions we've performed out of ignorance—causes we initiated that have brought the unavoidable consequences of current effect? Yogananda taught that Kriya Yoga can hasten the burning of past karmas. The ungerminated seeds of karma can be roasted during Kriya practice by the strong current of energy that rises up the inner spine. This inner fire ceremony is reflected in the fire ceremony practiced in India, in which grains of rice are offered into the flames, to symbolically burn up seeds of past bad karma.

A friend told me of an experience that perfectly illustrated this principle. While practicing Kriya, certain unpleasant memories of the past would suddenly arise. She wondered, "Was I doing something wrong?"

When I asked if those memories returned during her practice, she replied, "No, in fact, those negative memories never came back again." Far from doing something wrong, she was doing something right! Her Kriya Yoga practice was releasing those old hurts once and for all. The memories themselves were expressions of the *chitta vrittis* mentioned earlier, burned up forever in the fire of devotional Kriya Yoga practice.

Not all past karmas can be worked out so quickly and easily. Some are given to help us learn important lessons. The consequences of wrong actions coming as karma are *not* sent to punish us. God is not a tyrannical judge, waiting to slap us the moment we do something wrong. The One who created us knows how difficult it is to overcome wrong desires and actions—He is a God of love and mercy, not of wrath and vengeance.

This truth was made clear to me once while driving in

India. At the long traffic lights, it is common to see beggars and others selling various items to those waiting in their cars. At a stoplight one day, I watched a very elderly man. He seemed to be both physically and mentally disabled. For some reason, his plight moved me intensely.

Praying and talking to God as Divine Mother, I found myself chastising Her with a combination of hurt, love, and some humor. "Don't you see Your child who is suffering here! Why don't You take care of him? I think You had too many children and have forgotten most of them! Don't You know there are ways to prevent that? What were You thinking?"

To my surprise, I instantly felt an answer in my heart, an answer that came with a deep sense of blessing. What I heard was not a voice speaking in my ears, but a silent answer speaking through my intuition. I still find Her words thrilling, alive with love and meaning. Her words were specific and deeply loving: "I give each one exactly what they need."

"I give *each one*": God is infinitely vast and impersonal, and at the same time personally aware of *each* one of us.

"*. . . exactly . . .*": God gives us the *exact* training each of us needs.

"*. . . what they need.*": These tests come not to punish, but because we *need* them to learn a helpful lesson or to develop an essential quality.

Perhaps the man had been scornful of others' weaknesses in another life. Perhaps he had lacked proper respect for his God-given body and mind and had neglected them through wrong living.

Whatever the cause, Divine Mother's response left me

with no doubt that what he was enduring was helping him to learn some vital lesson. Of course, I prayed for him, since I could offer no other help in that moment.

It is important to remember that such an impersonal understanding is not helpful advice, given to those in the midst of suffering. Our duty is, instead, to express kindness and compassion to those who are suffering.

When I've applied Divine Mother's guidance in my own life, I gain so much more from my tests. Doing so opens a door for me to feel the support and encouragement of a loving God during every challenge. Although it is not always easy to feel God's presence in each test, I've learned to trust that, whether I feel it or not, *God's help is there*.

When you respond to tests not from the emotional reactive process, but with detachment, calmness, and inner strength, you will sail through even the most difficult tests. You will also stop generating new karmic seeds born of the emotional desire for things to be different.

Finally, understand that God and the great saints *are on our side*. They want to help free us. They have waited a very long time for us to cooperate with their grace. When we can do so, their help is instantaneous and life-changing.

The complexity of karmic patterns in human life makes virtually every honest activity a *dharmic* duty for someone. The menial task of street sweeping may, for most people, be simply a paying job and a social necessity. However, it may be a karmic duty for some people—if, for example, the sweeper lived in a past incarnation in idle squalor. The exalted job of president of a large corporation might be merely a burden for some people, and a cause of further karmic involvement, owing (perhaps) to a lurking desire for self-importance. For one, however, who treats that position as an opportunity to serve others, or to promote a good cause, it can be a step toward liberation from ego.

— SWAMI KRIYANANDA, *The Essence of the Bhagavad Gita*

CHAPTER ELEVEN

Change Your Destiny

Forget the past. The vanished lives of all men are dark with many shames. Human conduct is ever unreliable until anchored in the Divine. Everything in future will improve if you are making a spiritual effort now.

— SWAMI SRI YUKTESWAR, QUOTED IN *Autobiography of a Yogi*

Yogananda quoted Sri Yukteswar's words as the most helpful statement in his entire autobiography. They are at once consoling and encouraging. Consoling, because we've all made mistakes in the past, and we are bound to make more until we are fully anchored in the Divine. The greatest saints and masters have all erred on the long journey to freedom. Sri Yukteswar is advising us that guilt and regret are not helpful.

The words are encouraging because they remind us that we *can* gain control of our destiny, simply by making the right spiritual effort now. His promise is supported by

Krishna's advice in the Bhagavad Gita (2:40):

> In this path (of yoga action) there is no danger of
> "unfinished business," nor are there latent within
> it the opposite, canceling effects of duality.

Actions performed for selfish gain always have a karmic rebound. Spiritual effort—any selfless action—is different. Such actions are only liberating. Don't worry about all the karma you must still work out or any mistakes you have made. Instead, begin making a spiritual effort now.

People mistakenly think of their destiny as fixed and out of their control. I've heard people claim belief in a fixed destiny as an excuse for not taking proper precautions during times that call for it: "If it's my destiny to die, I'll die, so why bother being careful."

That way of thinking is true only in this way: if you don't look both ways before crossing a busy street, you may well be run over and killed. Yes, it *was* your destiny—but you *chose* that destiny by choosing to ignore common sense.

Our destiny is always a choice that we make, now or in the past.

What of those past karmas, those destinies, that still must come to us? Can we head them off before they reach us? Can we mitigate their effects?

Swami Kriyananda once gave me some helpful advice about a past karma that nearly led to my death. In 1999, when I still practiced some mountain climbing, I was descending a very steep and icy slope. Suddenly a boulder came crashing down the mountain and smashed into my leg. I could only stumble and crawl for the next hour as I sought help.

Although I had been alone on that part of the mountain, I miraculously found some other climbers and was soon being airlifted to a hospital. That was the end of my mountain climbing career! Soon after, Kriyananda remarked that if you have the karmic destiny to die by getting hit by a boulder falling off a precipice, then for the time being you should avoid being under precipices!

But then came the important message: In the meantime, he said, work on increasing your magnetism.

Once your magnetism is strong enough, the same karma may cause only a minor injury instead of death. Our magnetism is a protective aura, like a force field around us. When, for example, a cold virus is spreading around the community, a person who is run down, or whose immune system is weakened, will be more likely to catch the virus. Those with a strong immune system will stay relatively healthier.

Negative thoughts similarly weaken our magnetism, and can make us more vulnerable to catching the negativity in the world.

Increasing our magnetism is the best protection against receiving the full effects of past bad karma. It also attracts the help we need, including the right people and circumstances. A strong magnetic field can change our karmic destiny. Kriya Yoga, because it goes to the very heart of our magnetism, in our inner self, is the most effective tool to help us develop that protective shield.

Strong willpower too can help us change our destiny. Yogananda taught that, ". . . when you can control your destiny by your willpower, then you can do tremendous things."

When I moved to Ananda Village in 1977 I was drawn to the energy and joy I saw in the people there. I didn't foresee the tremendous growth of Ananda that later came. Most of us were living in small trailers and teepees—the previous year a fire had burnt down nearly all the homes. We must have seemed, to worldly eyes, a rag-tag, poor, unskilled group of naive idealists.

How to account for the dramatic change in this humble group into what is now a worldwide spiritual movement numbering many thousands? The power behind the transformation lies in the principles of Kriya Yoga. Looking at photographs of myself and others, "before Kriya Yoga" and "after Kriya Yoga," I can say that without exception the change is as clear as between night and day. Yogananda said we won't even recognize ourselves after learning and practicing Kriya Yoga.

A basic principle of Kriya is worth repeating. When we think more of giving to others and to God, and less of "looking out for number one" (ourselves), we find that somehow things begin working out for our own highest good—our destiny begins to change.

A beautiful story told by the Indian author and poet Rabindranath Tagore illustrates this truth:

> A very impoverished man, the story goes, lived in a simple village with his wife and children. One day he saw a grand procession traveling on the main road toward the village. When he saw the King of the country approaching with

his retinue, he couldn't believe his eyes. Here was his once-in-a-lifetime chance to ask for help from the wealthiest man in the kingdom.

As the king's carriage approached, the man stood at the side of the road and held his hand out for a donation. To his surprise, the carriage halted, and the king stepped out and approached him! It was indeed a life-changing moment for him. To his stunned surprise, the king asked him, "What do you have to give to *me*?"

The poor man reached into his pockets. All he had was a bundle of rice grains that he had bought for the family's meal. He gave the king one single grain of rice.

That night when he reached home, he took out the rice to prepare for cooking. Imagine his surprise when he discovered that among the grains of rice was one that had turned into pure gold. Imagine his dismay: "Oh, what a fool I was! I should have given him all that I had!"

Whatever we give to God—including our very life—becomes sanctified. It isn't that God needs anything. The spiritual law of giving and self-offering is for *our* benefit. It is the surest way to change our destiny.

Yes, we *can* change our destiny! Who else but we have created the circumstances of our present existence? Begin making more of the right spiritual effort now, and *everything* in the future will improve. The way forward is that simple.

Please remember that all suffering is in the last analysis self-generated. God doesn't will it on us. It comes as a result of the misuse of our own will, whether recently or in the distant past. Suffering can be banished by the right use of will. As Sri Yukteswar said, "Forget the past. The vanished lives of all men are dark with many shames. Everything in future will improve if you are making a spiritual effort now."

Don't think in terms of doing one thing big enough to lift you out of your present state. Think rather in terms of taking one step at a time. Commit yourself to some positive act, however small, and carry that act through to completion. Finish whatever you start.

When you make the right effort, and then invoke God's power to sustain you in that effort, you will find Him reinforcing you and giving you the strength gradually to win out over all obstacles. But you must make the right effort first. God cannot help you until you, yourself, first try your best.

— SWAMI KRIYANANDA, *In Divine Friendship*

CHAPTER TWELVE

The Goal: Self-Realization

The *Upanishads* have minutely classified every stage of spiritual advancement. A *siddha* ("perfected being") has progressed from the state of a *jivanmukta* ("freed while living") to that of a *paramukta* ("supremely free"—full power over death); the latter has completely escaped from the *mayic* thralldom and its reincarnational round. The *paramukta* therefore seldom returns to a physical body; if he does, he is an avatar, a divinely appointed medium of supernal blessings on the world.

— PARAMHANSA YOGANANDA, *Autobiography of a Yogi*

When I read *Autobiography of a Yogi* for the first time, the notion that I could become free from all suffering seemed the most attractive thing in the world. Yogananda's encouraging way of writing about *samadhi* made me think, "Yes, I can do this! It sounds easy!"

After living in India for several years, I've seen that my naïve belief that freedom is so easily attained has one clear advantage. People who grow up understanding the difficulty of the spiritual path often doubt their ability to succeed, "It's too hard—why try?"

To encourage us, Swami Kriyananda often recounted a story that Yogananda told:

> Paramhansa Yogananda, when a boy, had a vision in which he saw himself standing in the dusty marketplace of a Himalayan village. The scene around him roiled with the noise of people, confusion, the turmoil of conflicting ambitions and desires, and the urgency of self-interest. Dogs ran everywhere. Monkeys clambered down from roofs to snatch at food from the stalls. People protested loudly at whatever prices they were offered.
>
> Every now and then someone would pause before young Mukunda (as he was then known) and gaze at a spot somewhere behind him. A look of inexpressible yearning would come over that person's face. Then he would turn away again, and mutter sorrowfully, "Oh, but it's much too high for me!" That person would then turn back again to the hot, dusty marketplace and re-assume his link with the world around him.
>
> The same thing happened several times. At last, young Mukunda turned around to see what had awakened such deep longing in those few people. There behind him he beheld a high

mountain, at the top of which he saw, spread out invitingly, a large, enchantingly beautiful garden. What a thrilling contrast it made to the heat, the noise, the dirt, the confusion in the busy village around him!

His first thought was what those persons had expressed: "Oh, but it's much too high for me!" But then came a sterner thought: "Well, I can at least put one foot in front of the other!" Armed with determination, he set out to climb the mountain. The trek took a long time, but at last he arrived at, and joyfully entered into the paradise garden at the top.

If you are reading this book, you may have had a glimpse of that high mountain. Ask yourself right now, "Am I content to remain in the dusty marketplace?"

Yes, it is difficult. We have karma, desires, attachments, all holding us back. We have a body that often makes it difficult to overcome our identification with matter.

But there is hope! I've seen again and again: those who begin taking one step after another on the path to freedom can make great progress in one lifetime—they can even reach the goal described by Yogananda.

Most people don't realize that a deep yearning for freedom means they are already close to the end of the journey. When a disciple of Yogananda was discouraged by difficulties, he lamented, "Sir, I don't think I have very good karma." Yogananda spoke to him fiercely, "Remember this. It takes very, *very*, VERY good karma even to *want* to know God!"

We are on a journey of many lifetimes, perhaps millions of lives. By the time we have reached this point, we are far closer to the end of the journey than we realize. Don't give up now!

Paramhansa Yogananda told the following story to help us understand that we are free already, and that we only need to reclaim our freedom.

A pregnant lioness had grown large with her unborn cub, when one day, feeling weak from lack of food, she spied a flock of sheep—easy prey! But when she bounded into the flock, the unborn cub emerged and dropped to the ground. In the exertion of the moment, the mother lion didn't realize that she had lost her offspring, so she wandered away to enjoy her meal, leaving the defenseless cub behind.

When the flock had recovered from the frightful attack, they discovered the cute lion cub crying for its mother, and a mother sheep took pity on it and resolved to raise it as her own.

Growing up surrounded by sheep, the lion learned to bleat like the flock and to graze on grass. Like his brethren, he learned to be timid and fearful, even as his body swelled into the form of a powerful adult lion.

A magnificent lion leader, a veritable king of the jungle, chanced upon the flock one day, and as he readied himself for the kill, he couldn't believe his eyes! There, huddled with the flock, was a lion, fainting from fear and bleating like the sheep around him!

Thoroughly puzzled, the lion king approached. "What's the matter with you?! Why do you, my brother, fear me like a frightened sheep?" The timid sheep-lion pleaded, "Please don't kill me! I'm just a helpless sheep!"

The lion king finally understood. Seizing the young lion by the scruff of his neck and dragging him to a nearby pool of water, he exhorted him scornfully, "Look at your reflection! You aren't a sheep! You are a mighty lion!" Seeing his reflection side by side with the lion king's, the young lion at last felt his fear fall from him.

Years of delusion having dropped away, he learned to roar like a lion, knowing that he had never been a sheep. And so he reclaimed his true nature.

We, too, have been fooled; we have forgotten who and what we really are. Now at last we are waking up to our true nature. The Indian sage Patanjali refers to that awakening as *smriti* — memory. We don't have to learn it, earn it, or acquire it. When we awaken in divine bliss, we experience our true nature as deeply familiar — *remembered* with perfect clarity.

True awakening is not easy, nor is it a trick of the mind that can be dissolved only by thinking it so. Reclaiming our lost inheritance is the only battle that has ever mattered throughout our many lives. It is the journey of every soul to find perfect freedom. Every day, we have a choice before us: will we prolong our suffering, or will we make the effort to transcend it forever?

One day I received a phone call from a man inquiring about learning Kriya Yoga through Ananda. He asked me, "Using your practices, how long will it take me to reach samadhi and final freedom?"

I explained that the length of the journey depends on many things, including our individual karma, the purity of our heart, and our effort. It could easily take the remainder of this life, and beyond.

Unhappy with the "product" I was offering, he complained, "I called this other group that teaches Kriya, and they said I could reach samadhi in six weeks if I attend their seminar! Do you mean to say you can't do better than that?"

Further discussion told me that he wasn't interested in investing much effort. I suggested that he accept the other group's offer and test whether their claims were true.

The spiritual path is not easy. But with the right effort, the right teacher and teaching, the right attitude of heart, and with a sustained practice, the sincere seeker can reach freedom, one step at a time.

"Divine freedom," Swami Kriyananda writes in *The New Path*, "comes only with the attainment of *nirbikalpa samadhi*. . . . Only with *nirbikalpa samadhi* does one become what is known as a *jivan mukta*, free even while living in a physical body."

A *jivan mukta* may still have past karma to work out, but he is free from ego bondage and its motivations, so he cannot create new karma. In this state, one can quickly and easily work out all past karmas, even during meditation. Make becoming a *jivan mukta* your goal in life. What if you fall short of that goal? You will see that any gains you make in this lifetime will carry you quickly toward the divine shores.

People often lament, "I have too much karma to become free," or "I have this particular karma, and I need to work it out first before taking up the spiritual path in earnest."

Friend, we've been wandering for many, many lifetimes with that same thought, "I just need to work out this desire, or that karma, before finding freedom." That approach leads only to more wandering.

It will help us to remember that even a *jivan mukta* is not free of all karma, but is free from the bondage that karma brings and from the desires and attachments that lead to further witless actions and the creation of new karma. Such a one still lives in this world of action but is inwardly untouched by its effects.

The greatest challenge facing every seeker is to overcome desire. What should we do, when our desires and yearnings continue to engulf us? We should at least *try* to live as if we were free. A Kriya Yogi friend told me that his New Year's resolution was to act during that year as if he were a *jivan mukta*. When facing any important decision, he would ask, "What would a *jivan mukta* do?"

I could see that my friend, who is responsible for leading and helping many people, received excellent results with that practice. In a way, *jivan mukta* is what we already are and always have been. Why not reclaim our memory of that lost birthright now? The key is that our actions are no longer guided by ego-motivation. To the degree that we can do so even now, we are free.

Karna, one of the main characters in the *Mahabharata*, was burdened by the results of his past wrong decisions. His story shows how we can find freedom even in our present circumstances.

A long series of events have led to a final battle between Arjuna, the perfect disciple of the Lord as Krishna, and Karna, who has a mixture of good and evil tendencies—much like most of us. Krishna explains that although Karna has been pierced by arrows, he cannot be defeated until he has used up all of his good karma.

To help his beloved disciple Arjuna, Krishna disguises himself as a wandering holy man, and approaches Karna as though seeking alms. Knowing that Karna has none of the traditional gifts to give him, and knowing that Karna is generous to a fault, Krishna asks him to give all the spiritual good karma he has ever earned.

Likely understanding that it is the Lord Himself approaching him in disguise, Karna replies by offering Krishna not only all the spiritual merit he has gained in the past, but all that he is currently earning, and all that he will gain in the future. Such is the greatness of Karna's generosity! As we soon see, it will be his saving grace.

But Krishna wants even more. Knowing that Karna has no water to bless his gift in the prescribed way, Krishna insists that he still follow the ritual form of giving. Karna then removes one of the arrows sticking into his body and blesses the gift with his own blood.

Collapsing from weakness, Karna closes his eyes. Suddenly he feels drops of refreshing water falling on him. Opening his eyes, he sees only the Lord, now in His full splendor, tears of compassion flowing from his eyes. With divine love, Krishna tells Karna that his generosity has pleased him greatly and that his sins are washed away. Krishna says, "Ask for any boon, and I will give it to you."

What would you ask for if God offered to grant you any wish? Think about it for a moment.

Karna's request is equally surprising and liberating. He asks only that in future lives, he again be selflessly willing to give to anyone whatever that one asks.

Krishna replies, "Your sins are insignificant when compared to the merit accrued by your charity and magnanimity. Your present suffering is due to those sins, but fear not, Karna. By your final act of surrendering even your merit to me, I myself shall take on the burden of your sins and will relieve you from your physical pain."

Krishna then tells Karna that he will never again have to reincarnate.

The lesson of the story is that we don't need to be perfect to reach the goal of freedom in God. Devotional self-offering, generosity of spirit, selflessness in our actions—all these are much more powerful than any faults that we may have. Do your best to live in that freedom, and you will find yourself arriving much more quickly on its shores.

Self-realization is the knowing in all parts of body, mind, and soul that you are now in possession of the kingdom of God; that you do not have to pray that it come to you; that God's omnipresence is your omnipresence; and that all that you need to do is improve your knowing.

— PARAMHANSA YOGANANDA, *The Essence of Self-Realization*

CHAPTER THIRTEEN

Transcending the Ego

"Which is greater," one may ask, "a swami or a yogi?" If and when final oneness with God is achieved, the distinctions of the various paths disappear. The Bhagavad Gita, however, points out that the methods of yoga are all-embracive. Its techniques are not meant only for certain types and temperaments, such as those few who incline toward the monastic life; yoga requires no formal allegiance. Because the yogic science satisfies a universal need, it has a natural universal applicability.

A true yogi may remain dutifully in the world; there he is like butter on water, and not like the easily-diluted milk of unchurned and undisciplined humanity. To fulfill one's earthly responsibilities is indeed the higher path, provided the yogi, maintaining a mental uninvolvement with egotistical desires, plays his part as a willing instrument of God.

— PARAMHANSA YOGANANDA, *Autobiography of a Yogi*

Renunciation isn't a simple matter of changing the color of one's clothes (Swamis traditionally wear orange in India), forsaking a few things of the world, or taking a vow.

Renunciation means *inwardly* renouncing all egotistical desires and self-definitions. In his autobiography, Yogananda even says that the life of the householder is a higher path to divine freedom than the life of the monastic, provided that the householder performs his worldly duties in a spirit of detachment from the results.

Formal and only outward renunciation, on the other hand, can lead to spiritual pride, something I've seen first-hand. On the positive side, practicing ego-transcendence as a monk or as a nun *can* be helpful—it can greatly hasten spiritual progress for those suited to that life.

Swami Kriyananda's approach to renunciation was positive—bliss-affirming rather than life-negating. That positive approach included many of the attitudes shared in this book, especially the offering of our thoughts, actions, and motivations to God.

Selflessness can, by itself, lead to divine joy. I learned this priceless lesson during a late night spent in a hospital emergency room. For several days, I had experienced pain in my side that suddenly increased alarmingly, to the point where medical treatment seemed in order. It was near midnight on a Saturday, when American hospitals tend to be very busy treating alcohol or drug-related injuries and overdoses. On this particular night, the emergency room was filled to capacity.

The doctor who received me decided that my pain, indeed, needed urgent care. He led me to a room where several other patients were waiting. By this time, the pain was so intense that I could only lie curled on the bed, clutching my side.

As I lay there, I overheard a doctor who was trying to save the life of a young man who had overdosed on drugs. When I turned to where the unconscious teenager was lying, I saw the anguished face of his girlfriend, who began pleading, "Please come back! Don't die!"

Absorbed in the compassion I felt for the boy's much greater suffering, my own pain seemed trivial. Compassion inspired prayer: I asked God to bring him back and give him another chance. I also prayed for the girl, that her heart be strengthened for whatever might come.

Almost instantly, I felt a joy that, for the rest of that night, helped me transcend all pain.

Before long, I was moved away for some tests. I never learned what happened to the boy. The tests showed that even though the pain had vanished, my gallbladder would have to be removed. To this day, I see myself as the beneficiary of an excellent trade: my gallbladder in exchange for what I could not have received otherwise—a divine lesson.

To the extent we practice selflessness, we will feel a corresponding inner freedom and joy. When our selflessness becomes complete devotional offering to God, our joy will become divine joy.

Swami Kriyananda gave a number of practical tips for transcending the ego, central to our way of life in Ananda's monastery in India. Although he directed his book, *Sadhu, Beware!*, to monks and nuns, the principles he outlines are helpful for all. When people ask me which books I most recommend for Kriya Yogis, I always mention *Sadhu, Beware!* (in addition to Yogananda's *Autobiography of a Yogi* and Swami Kriyananda's *The Essence of the Bhagavad Gita*).

Kriyananda explains the importance of ego-|transcendence for everyone:

> The first duty of every soul is to release the hold that ego-consciousness has upon it. All other spiritual practices are subservient to this one supreme obligation. I address ego-transcendence, therefore, as the first, and indeed the only, challenge on the spiritual path, whether one be a renunciate, a householder, or living for God in some other way.

> — SWAMI KRIYANANDA, *Sadhu, Beware!*

Sadhu, Beware! gives thirty-three techniques for becoming an "ego-detective"—individually and collectively helping us to root out the influence of ego. I'll share a few of them here:

> #2. When people fail to credit you for something you did and did well, say nothing. In your heart, however, give all the credit to God.

> #21. It is not humility to tell yourself, "I can't. ..." Remember, God can do anything. If you give Him the chance, moreover, He can do anything

through you. Ask Him for the inspiration, the guidance, and the strength to do whatever you must do. As Yogananda put it, "Pray in this way: I will reason; I will will; I will act — but guide Thou my reason, will, and activity in everything I do."

#32. Don't let your mind play with the thought of where and how you yourself fit into any picture. Don't toy with flattery by entertaining it even lightly in your mind. Reject sternly any thought of self-importance, self-praise, self-justification, and blame.

This subject is as important for you as your own salvation, for your spiritual liberation depends upon release from ego-consciousness.

It is interesting that all but three of the thirty-three tools deal with how we can relate more selflessly and impersonally to others, as well as to their thoughts about us, and our place within a group.

Our relationships with close family, friends, and co-workers are the easiest way to see what we still need to work on to loosen the grip of the ego. The practice of ego-transcendence is for everyone — householders as well as monastics.

I find it helpful to practice the techniques as a game. If we follow them with too much sense of self-importance, we may reinforce the very ego we are trying to transcend. When my inner ego-detective catches "my" ego responding with self-justification, for example, I find it best to laugh delightedly: "Aha!—Caught you!"—and lightly move on with a sense of inner freedom.

Patanjali defined yoga as *"yogas chitta vritti nirodh"*— "Yoga is the neutralization of the *vrittis* (vortices) of *chitta* (emotional, ego-attached feelings)." He defined feeling as one of four aspects of human consciousness: *mon* (mind); *buddhi* (intellect); *ahankara* (ego); *chitta* (feeling).

To clarify these four aspects, Paramhansa Yogananda gave the example of the image of a horse reflected in a mirror. *Mon* (mind) receives the image through the physical senses but does not define or analyze it. *Buddhi* (intellect) defines what is being perceived, in this case "a horse." *Ahankara* (ego) identifies it as *my* horse. Even at this point there is no real bondage—as a description "my horse" is abstract and not yet emotional.

It is at the point that *chitta* (feeling) enters the picture that we become caught in bondage. With strong emotional feeling it cries out, "I *like* my horse! How *happy* I am to see my horse!" Feeling alone is what binds the ego in delusion. By calming the agitated feelings of the heart and gaining control of the reactive process, the ego becomes free, no longer bound.

We cannot find freedom by attempting to kill the ego. The ego cannot be killed. In *Samadhi*, the poem about his first experience of cosmic consciousness, Yogananda wrote: "I, the Cosmic Sea, watch the little ego floating in me."

When the purified heart offers the ego completely back to God, the yogi becomes one with the cosmic sea. Then the little ego, still alive, is seen as part of that sea, no longer as something separate.

I've had the opportunity in this life to practice ego-transcendence as a monk and as a householder. Both approaches have advantages and disadvantages. Unless we approach the householder life in the spirit that Yogananda described, "maintaining a mental uninvolvement with egotistical desires, plays his part as a willing instrument of God," we may find ourselves becoming further enmeshed in desires and restlessness. On the other hand, approached in a spirit of renunciation and service, the householder life can give us priceless training in self-offering, as we learn to sacrifice personal needs for those of others.

The life of a monk, too, has its pluses and minuses. The monastic life can reinforce ego-involvement when we succumb to the temptation to put our own needs first—especially when those needs are proudly rationalized as being "spiritual." On the positive side, the monastic lifestyle can provide us many opportunities to give one's life more completely to the welfare of all—in both meditation and service.

The color and style of our clothing, monastic or householder, is not as important as the inner garb of ego-transcendence. Others cannot see that color easily, but God can. Wherever God has placed us, make ego-transcendence our daily habit and our life's goal.

Ego-transcendence is the very essence of spiritual progress. One wonders why so little teaching has been devoted to it, and so much more emphasis has been placed on ego-suppression. One wonders also why, especially among renunciates, so much attention has been given to indirect efforts such as eliminating attachments and desires. Naturally these self-limitations must be renounced also, the energy formerly committed to them channeled upward unidirectionally to the brain and the spiritual eye between the eyebrows. I can only think that the reason ego-transcendence has received so little attention is that most people during *Kali Yuga* could not comprehend that the ego really has no existence except in its fleeting dream-reality. This brief seeming is only (as my Guru said) like a glimmer of sunlight reflected in a sliver of glass on the roadside.

— SWAMI KRIYANANDA, *A Renunciate Order for the New Age*

CHAPTER FOURTEEN

The Need for a Guide

Because of certain ancient yogic injunctions, I cannot give a full explanation of *Kriya Yoga* in the pages of a book intended for the general public. The actual technique must be learned from a *Kriyaban* or *Kriya Yogi*; here, a broad reference must suffice.

— PARAMHANSA YOGANANDA, *Autobiography of a Yogi*

Yogananda, in the chapter on Kriya Yoga in his autobiography, repeatedly emphasizes that the technique of Kriya Yoga cannot be separated from the disciple-guru relationship. Thus, he notes that Lahiri Mahasaya "received [Kriya] from his guru"—just as Krishna gave the technique to his disciple Arjuna. He states that the disciples of Christ, including St. Paul, practiced Kriya or a similar technique, and that Kriya Yoga must be practiced "with the guidance of a guru."

The internet has made it easier for people to find their destined path, but it has also led to a lot of confusion and false advice. I have witnessed an amazing degree of misinformation and faulty guidance about Kriya as a result, especially from people who claim to have learned the holy technique "on the internet" instead of from a qualified teacher or guru.

The internet makes a very poor guru! It includes proud claims by some that *only* their approach to Kriya is correct. The fallacy of such claims lies in the notion that the technique is mechanical in giving results.

Early in the internet era, 1997, I began managing the worldwide Ananda website. I soon found myself responding to emails that asked, in confusion, "Which Kriya technique is the real one, and where should I learn it?" My answer, then as now, is: "The right Kriya Yoga technique is the one your guru gives you. First find your path and teacher, then learn Kriya from them."

What is the best way to find your teacher and path? The followers are often the best test of the effectiveness of a teacher and teaching. When you meet followers of a Kriya path, try to discern whether they are developing spiritual qualities of kindness, energy, humility, clarity, joy, and purity of heart.

Try also to feel with calm intuition whether the teacher or guru is the right one for you. Those answers can only come from within, through sincere inquiry.

If you still aren't sure, take a tentative step forward, perhaps trying the practices and watching the results. I've witnessed the life-changing benefits of Kriya practice in the lives of thousands of seekers who've learned the sacred technique through Ananda Sangha. I can unreservedly recommend this path. Please know that such a life-changing step should never be taken lightly.

Before reading *Autobiography of a Yogi*, I tried to follow the spiritual path on my own, guided by books. At first, I didn't understand the need for a guru to serve as a master-guide to the spiritual life. My initial and sincere intention was to try to live as a hermit.

I would save up some money and go into California's mountain wilderness for weeks at a time to live alone, sleeping outdoors, and eating simply from the supplies I brought with me. The days found me roaming the hills, keeping my mind and heart on God to the best of my ability — though it was never as much as I wanted. The nights found me sleeping under the vast blanket of stars, gazing up at the infinite universe.

My only outward company were the animals. On one freezing-cold morning, I was brought out of sleep by someone or something gently playing with my long wild hair. With the top of my head barely out of my sleeping bag, I realized that there were two tiny birds chirping and flitting about in my hair. I think they saw my long hair as potential material for their nest!

Despite experiencing the spiritual romance of the hermit life, I could tell that I was making little spiritual progress. In my effort to get away from the restless crowds of the city, I discovered to my chagrin that there was one very restless person who followed me everywhere I went. He would not leave me alone. It was that fellow Devarshi, chattering mentally and flitting about like the two small birds! I realized that I needed three things: a wise guru-advisor, the support and company of fellow truth-seekers, and a true spiritual teaching.

In the American legal system, we are allowed to represent ourselves as our own lawyer, even if we have no legal training and are not licensed as attorneys. A common saying in the legal profession is that those who represent themselves in court have a fool for a lawyer. And—well—I had a fool for a guru!

Soon after, I began following Yogananda's teachings and moved to Ananda Village. My heart's prayers for a worthy guide were answered. There I found everything I'd been seeking: a guru in Yogananda, wise guides and teachers, and the company of fellow seekers.

There is a saying in India, universally true, "When the disciple is ready, the guru appears." When our hearts are filled with sincere longing for God, we attract a true teacher.

During Kriya Yoga initiation ceremonies, Swami Kriyananda gave primary importance to tuning in to the power and magnetism of the Guru, even while practicing the Kriya technique. In the following passage, he explains why Kriya is given as an initiation, and not merely a technique.

> Kriya Yoga, in order to be wholly effective, must be received not only intellectually (in written or spoken form), but *vibrationally*, in the form of initiation. A magnet is created either by electrical realignment of the molecules, or by close proximity to another magnet. Attunement with a God-awakened guru influences the *samskaras* (comparable to the material molecules) to flow

upward to the brain.

We are dealing here with a reality subtler, and much more difficult to master, than mere molecules of metal. Without an experienced guide, even mountain climbing can be fatal—though death, in this case, only ends a single incarnation. Spiritual mistakes can be costlier, in terms of long-range suffering.

Proximity to a master's spiritual power changes us in the way that a powerful magnet can transform an ordinary piece of iron into a magnet.

I noticed the whimsical operation of this principle in a cup that was designed to hold paper clips. At the top, there was a small hole to receive the clips. The hole was lined with a magnetic ring that kept several clips easily accessible at the top of the container. Whenever I removed a clip, several others would trail along, stuck to the first one. The clips had become magnetized by proximity to the stronger magnet at the circular opening.

A strong magnet always affects a weaker one. In the company of a saint, we are changed by the saint's powerful magnetism. Divine healings often occur through the power of a saint's magnetism. At the same time, it's important to recognize that we cannot receive spiritual magnetism if we are only passively receptive, like those magnetized paper clips. What's needed, instead, is a positive, calm, dynamic receptivity. This is what Yogananda called *attunement* to the Guru's magnetism. The Master often urged his disciples, "Stay in tune, stay in tune!"

In *Autobiography of a Yogi*, Paramhansa Yogananda tells how he received the experience of cosmic consciousness through the touch of his guru, Sri Yukteswar. That touch came after Yogananda first fled his guru's ashram to find God in solitary meditation in the Himalayas. Only after returning to his guru, with "shamefacedness," was he able to receive that touch of grace.

So important is the principle of attunement that Yogananda included the following line in his poetic description of samadhi: "By deeper, longer, thirsty, guru-given meditation comes this celestial *samadhi*."*

We don't need to be in the guru's physical presence in order to receive his magnetic blessings. By consciously thinking of the guru with an open heart, we can draw the guru's power to us.

After spending several weeks with Swami Kriyananda in India, I once asked for his advice shortly before I returned to America. I said, "It's easy to feel attunement with Master [Yogananda] in your presence, Swamiji. How can we feel that way in our everyday lives?" He answered:

> "What I do is ask myself, 'Master, what would you do? What do you want me to do?' I ask both those questions. For instance, in writing the [*Essence of the Bhagavad*] *Gita*, I feel a real joy inside, as if Master is saying, 'This is what I want you to do.' So, it is not enough to just pray and meditate. We need to ask Master, 'How would you handle this?'
>
> "Also, I have found that (mentally) chanting

* This line was edited out of later editions of *Autobiography of a Yogi*.

'AUM Guru' is a wonderful practice. If you keep that consciousness day and night, it's amazing how you can change. You feel more and more desire for God, more and more purity of heart, more and more dedication. That's what really matters."

I've found those two pieces of advice to be the most important he ever gave me. The first is to ask the guru to guide all our actions and thoughts. Over the years, this practice begins to develop an ability to feel the guru's guidance more and more easily through our intuition. The simple act of asking for his help, by itself, makes us receptive to his help. Equally important, as we attune ourselves inwardly to him, our own magnetism will strengthen and grow.

This practice has helped guide me in making difficult decisions as well as in offering guidance to others. We can ask the guru for his guidance in all things—in every aspect of our lives: our relationships, work, health, and so on, without exception. The guru *wants* to help us in every circumstance. He is *waiting* for us to make the soul call asking for his help.

The second part of that advice, equally life-changing, has been the practice of mentally chanting "AUM Guru" throughout the day while walking, at idle moments, while falling asleep, waking up—as often as I can remember. I now find the mental chanting continuing by itself at times, even during sleep.

It is so simple—why not give it a try? If you could take a magic pill that would give you "more and more desire for God, more and more purity of heart, more and more dedication," wouldn't you take it eagerly? Those are the qualities that matter most.

Another gem of advice that Kriyananda often shared with us is to find ways to serve the guru. When someone asked him, "What is your *sadhana* (spiritual practice)?" he unhesitatingly replied, "My sadhana is guru *bhakti*, guru *seva*, and meditation. And by doing those things, I am free."

Seva is a Sanskrit word that means "service." Those who are too aloof, or feel above the need to serve others, invariably feel stuck in their spiritual lives.

A guiding principle in my life, almost like a mantra, has been a phrase from *Autobiography of a Yogi*: "grateful service." Sri Yukteswar admonished the young Yogananda for certain "erroneous lessons" he had absorbed, that had led him into "agreeable delusions of irresponsibility."

His guru chided him:

> "Those who are too good for this world are adorning some other. So long as you breathe the free air of earth, you are under obligation to render grateful service. He alone who has fully mastered the breathless state is freed from cosmic imperatives. I will not fail to let you know when you have attained the final perfection."

You may recall the story of how I became stuck in quicksand. The friend who pulled me out played the symbolic role of the guru whom God sends to free us from the quicksand of delusion. To be saved, I needed only to cooperate with him. Cooperating with the guru, through attunement to him, by practicing his teachings, and by serving him are sure ways of cooperating with divine grace

The essence of the spiritual path is attunement. Devotees often insist, "God is the Guru. What need have I for a human guide?" God, however, does everything through instruments. Even the stars and planets were created by higher beings in attunement with His will. Yes, God is Omnipresence. Yes, He knows our least thought. He acts, however, through instruments. As the child needs teachers, even though all the information they teach is available to him, if he knows how to seek it, so the sincere seeker absolutely needs a guru.

— SWAMI KRIYANANDA, *Sadhu, Beware!*

CHAPTER FIFTEEN

The Technological Yogi

Referring to yoga's sure and methodical efficacy, Lord Krishna praises the technological yogi in the following words: "The yogi is greater than body-disciplining ascetics, greater even than the followers of the path of wisdom (*Jnana Yoga*), or of the path of action (*Karma Yoga*); be thou, O disciple Arjuna, a yogi!" [Bhagavad Gita, 6:46]

— PARAMHANSA YOGANANDA, *Autobiography of a Yogi*

What does Paramhansa Yogananda mean by "*technological* yogi." A common definition of *technology* is "the practical application of knowledge" in a certain field.

For best results, we need to understand the basic technology of Kriya. Knowing the yoga teachings is a first, though important step on the journey. The true technological yogi is one who also *practices* and *applies* that knowledge every day.

125

We've talked about the emotional reactive process and its relation to the breath. Yoga describes three main channels of energy that make up the *astral spine* (the subtle energy spine). The two outer channels are *iḍa* and *pingala*. The main central channel is the *sushumna*. The most important effect of advanced yoga techniques such as Kriya is that they enable us to withdraw our energy from the outer channels into the deeper channel of the *sushumna*.

We can observe the overall level of our energy by watching our moods and reactions. The movement of energy in the two outer spinal channels corresponds to our consciousness of *dwaita* (duality). Energy flows through the *iḍa* and *pingala* channels in its dualistic expression: action and reaction, positive and negative, happy and sad, up and down, cause and effect. When we can withdraw our consciousness into the *sushumna*, we enter divine states of inspiration, joy, love, and pure-hearted kindness.

Divine states have no equal and opposite reaction — we are one with the divine Truth beyond creation. Sometimes we may be fooled into thinking that an emotional high is divinely inspired. But if it is truly a divine state, it will not be followed by a counterbalancing emotional slump.

When we live only in our emotions, we experience a roller coaster ride of ups and downs — never-ending and often extreme. Giddy emotion can be enjoyable for a time, but it can be anguishing to experience its balancing opposite. The yogi discovers that outwardly happy emotions are a garish counterfeit of the incomparably more thrilling divine joy of deep meditation.

The Kriya technique helps us learn to control the life force and withdraw it from the dual outer channels into the single channel of the *sushumna*. Paramhansa Yogananda explained that spiritual progress doesn't begin until we start to enter the *sushumna*.

Swami Kriyananda advised Kriya Yogis to practice the technique as if we were already centered in the *sushumna*:

> The real [spiritual] awakening comes in the deep spine, so we want to visualize this energy as passing through the deep spine from the start. Don't think about the *iḍa* and *pingala* during Kriya, but think about the center of the spine, the *sushumna* channel, and visualize it as a hollow tube.

This advice is so central and universal to the spiritual life that it is equally valid for people who follow any true spiritual tradition. Practices that help us focus on the *iḍa* and *pingala* mainly serve as tools to develop our awareness of those channels, as a preliminary step toward the real goal of bringing our consciousness into the *sushumna*.

The two outer channels are associated with the physical breath. When we experience a surge of emotional happiness, the energy rises in the *iḍa* energy channel on the left side of the spine, often accompanied by a strong inhalation. When emotional happiness inevitably gives way to sadness, the energy descends in the *pingala* channel on the right side, accompanied by an exhalation—think of a sigh associated with disappointment.

Kriya—along with other breathing techniques that work with the inner energy—make use of the natural connection between the physical breath and the corresponding inner *astral breath*. Those techniques are practiced not only in the lungs but in the astral spine. The deepest effects of Kriya are experienced in the astral, energetic body, far more than in the physical body.

When my wife advised me (chapter six), "Detach yourself. Control the reactive process. Live the teachings," she wasn't telling me to detach myself from my human feelings or my soul connection with her. She was urging me to step aside from the emotional reactions of the *iḍa* and *pingala* and go deep within.

Swami Kriyananda explained that divine love has an impersonal side that can be difficult for humans to accept, accustomed as we are to emotional expressions of affection.

> The main — indeed, the only important thing on the spiritual path is to calm the emotions. Calm feeling is love, which unites the soul with God. Restless or agitated feelings, on the other hand — our emotions — disrupt our vision and prevent us from achieving full acceptance that in our true reality we are manifestations of the eternal stillness of God.

Divine love is expansive — large enough to embrace the well-being of all. But it does so impartially, without dual emotional expressions such as attraction and rejection, desire and anger.

In my wife's final days, I found that I could be a great deal more helpful when I was in a calm state of divine love, instead of being caught up in turbulent waves of human emotions. I was able, then, to serve as a channel for a higher, impersonal love, even when that love was *expressed*, at times, in personal ways. That calm divine love can be found in the *sushumna*, first in deep meditation, then in daily life.

The astral spine is where the energy centers known as the chakras are located. The chakras are like doorways through which the outflowing energy enmeshes us in desire, attachment, anger, and in reactions to outer events.

Kriya practice helps us counter the outflow of energy through the chakras by strengthening the divine current in the *sushumna*, thereby creating a powerful magnetism there. Great as the power of delusion is to draw us into the endless attractions "out there" in the world, Kriya Yoga can create such a powerful magnetism in the *sushumna* that the inner world becomes much more attractive than any worldly fascination.

Once centered in the *sushumna*, we no longer need to fight endless battles with desire and attraction. Our only need is to win the single battle of controlling the life force and generating an inner magnetism that will draw our spirit upward through the *sushumna*, into the bliss of our true nature.

When we have won that battle, we feel the divine joy within—all outer attractions fall away naturally, even easily. I've heard many Kriya Yogis testify to how they have overcome the bad habits of a lifetime through Kriya.

Few stories are as extreme as that of a man who was deeply addicted to alcohol when he met Paramhansa Yogananda. The Master urged him to practice Kriya and promised him that, in time, the joy of God would overcome the counterfeit high he received from drinking. One day while he was meditating with a whiskey bottle in one hand and his Kriya beads (for counting the number of Kriya breaths) in the other, he found a divine joy that completely banished his addiction. He never again felt a need for strong drink.

The inner magnetism generated by devoted Kriya practice also creates a powerful energy field around us—often called the *aura*. It is like an invisible umbrella that shields us from the rain of our past karma to an extent that would seem miraculous.

I once said to a great woman saint (Ananda Moyi Ma) in India, "All of us [my fellow disciples in America and I] feel great love for you." She replied with appreciation, but impersonally, "There is no love outside of God's love." And God's love is forever impersonal. This is to say that, although God cares deeply for all of us, individually, He wants nothing from us in return, and can wait for ages, if necessary, for us to return His love selflessly and merge back in Him. Human love is particular; it is for one person, or for a limited number of people. It cannot but be to some extent selfish. Being founded on the emotions, it is circumscribed by personal feelings. And it excludes from its reckoning the needs of mankind in general.

Only divine love is completely impersonal, impartial, self-giving, and concerned for the well-being of others.

— SWAMI KRIYANANDA, *A Renunciate Order for the New Age*

CHAPTER SIXTEEN

Inner Communion

The sage [Bhaduri Mahasaya] locked his vibrant body in the lotus posture. In his seventies, he displayed no unpleasing signs of age or sedentary life. Stalwart and straight, he was ideal in every respect. His face was that of a *rishi*, as described in the ancient texts. Noble-headed, abundantly bearded, he always sat firmly upright, his quiet eyes fixed on Omnipresence. The saint and I entered the meditative state. After an hour, his gentle voice roused me.

"You go often into the silence, but have you developed *anubhava*?"* He was reminding me to love God more than meditation. "Do not mistake the technique for the Goal."

— PARAMHANSA YOGANANDA, *Autobiography of a Yogi*

---

* Actual perception of God

What is *anubhava*, the actual perception of God? Does it mean having visions of the Lord in one form or another, or experiencing spiritual phenomena? Beginning meditators often too eagerly seek phenomena as the goal, or as the surest sign of spirituality.

Yogananda cautioned people not to seek experiences in meditation. He advised them that if such experiences come, to let them come and be grateful for them. Sometimes a "spiritual experience" may be only a projection of our subconscious mind. The test of a divine experience is that it changes us in real, lasting ways. Even so, Paramhansa Yogananda advised people not to talk to others about their spiritual experiences.

Swami Kriyananda tells a story of Trailanga Swami, a great saint mentioned in *Autobiography of a Yogi*.

> A devotee of his [Trailanga Swami] begged him repeatedly to bless him through that image [he had an image of the Divine Mother in his temple].
>
> One evening the two of them were seated together in the next room. The image itself walked in, sat down, and conversed with them on lofty topics. After some time, the "idol" left the room and returned to its customary position. The divine power left it.
>
> Trailanga looked at the devotee calmly and asked, "And now, what have you got?" That passing phenomenon had been inspiring, certainly, but had it changed the devotee to the extent of giving him God? As my guru was wont to say,

"The path to God is not a circus!" The important thing is that we change ourselves. In this respect especially, Buddha was completely right.

Nevertheless, visions can be a consolation, certainly, though they are no guarantee that the visionary is a saint.

Yogananda told his audiences that he hadn't come to dogmatize them with a new religion, or with new beliefs. "I want to help you," he said, "toward the attainment of actual experience of Him, through your daily practice of Kriya Yoga. *The time for knowing God has come!*"

Knowing God is far different from having an isolated vision of God, though a single true experience can help us on the way to that knowing. The deeper and permanent knowing comes in meditation through long practice of *inner communion* with God.

Actual perception of God is the goal — not the practice of techniques. Meditation techniques are like a car that is needed to take us to the ocean — we won't be able to have direct experience of the ocean until we get out of the car.

The *experience* of God is unique for everyone. Our path to inner communion will also be unique, varying with our nature, our needs, and how God calls us. Here lies the most creative part of a sitting meditation practice. Even though there are no techniques to hold our attention, we do not become passive. The actual experience of God is uplifting, clear, joyful, often exhilarating, and ever new.

The art of meditation becomes especially important after we have finished practicing the techniques during our sitting meditation time. Perception of God comes through intuition, the feeling-perception of the heart.

Swami Kriyananda urged us to sit at the end of our meditation for at least fifteen minutes without practicing techniques. How do we fill that time? Many meditators struggle during what seems like an unstructured time.

Below are some suggestions that may help you enjoy the time of inner communion. We've touched on most of them already. All of them are worth exploring, in your own way.

Prayer

Inner communion begins by developing a relationship with God. Prayer, or talking to God, is one side of that relationship. Meditation can be thought of as the practice of listening for God's response, with ever-increasing receptiveness.

Deep prayer requires interiorization, full attention, and speaking from the heart. Without some degree of interiorization, our prayer can easily become emotional rather than devotional. Emotional prayer can be a good starting point, but the more we take prayer within, the more we approach that point of stillness where God can be seen and felt.

Concentration, too, is necessary. Imagine approaching a friend to ask for something important. If, as you speak, you keep looking around distractedly at everything going on around you, will your friend take your request seriously? Give God your full attention during prayer.

Pray from the heart, not from the head. Pray like a child, without guile, and with the full expectation that your Heavenly Father or Divine Mother wants to help you. They are on your side! Yogananda spoke of offering God our "prayer demands." Don't be a beggar before God, but a divine child, lovingly demanding your birthright.

As we go deeper in prayer, our prayerful state will transcend all need for words. Here is the deepest form of prayer: "Oh, how maddening!" Yogananda wrote. "I can pray no more with words, but only with wistful yearning."

If you are getting started in prayer or you are wanting to deepen your prayer life, I heartily recommend Yogananda's book of prayer-poems, *Whispers from Eternity*. Many meditators make it a practice to read one of the poems from *Whispers* at the beginning of their daily meditation. Devotional chanting, discussed in chapter seven, is another effective way to offer our prayers to God.

Receptivity

"As many as received him, to them gave he power to become the sons of God" (John, 1:12).

Christ is reminding us of the importance of receptivity. Try to listen inwardly—to feel in your heart the touch of the Divine. Think of tuning a radio receiver to a particular station. The radio station's signal is being broadcast everywhere, but to receive it, we need to sensitively tune the dial.

When we are trying to tune in to God's "wavelength," we should remember that the heart is the receiving station where we can perceive His response. Spend time during every meditation as a spiritual receiving station. It can help to concentrate your attention at the heart center during this time, with eyes turned calmly upward. Feel the first glimmerings of joy as a pleasant sensation in the heart. Tune in more and more deeply until you are absorbed in that joy. Then offer that feeling upward. In this way you will be cooperating with grace.

Receptivity is not passive. It takes concentration, energy, and a conscious lifting of our heart's energy. Instead of passively and vaguely waiting for a response, invite God to come in a specific way. You can invite Him to come as one of the eight aspects of God that Paramhansa Yogananda describes: peace, calmness, light, sound, power, wisdom, love, bliss. Read his *Metaphysical Meditations* to receive the inspiration of his beautiful visualizations of these divine expressions.

Also fruitful are prayers offered to, and communion with, a saint, or your guru. Their magnetism can transform you. Swami Kriyananda encouraged us to feel that Paramhansa Yogananda's aura was merging with ours as we meditated. You can do this even while practicing your meditation techniques.

If you relate to God as Father or Mother, or as one of the many forms in which He has expressed Himself, you can pray to God in that form. Begin with the personal form you revere, then try to go beyond the image itself. View that form as a window onto eternity. Yogananda's chant to Kali, a form of Divine Mother commonly worshiped in Bengal, expresses a devotion that expands beyond the limited form to the formless Divine.

Who tells me Thou art dark, O my Mother Divine,
Thousands of suns and moons from Thy body do
   shine!

As Kali, the Divine Mother is portrayed as having dark
skin. Yogananda is playfully telling Her that he knows Her
truth—that She is not limited to that singular dark form
but is present beyond form in all creation.

A Christian saint, St. Teresa of Avila, had an experience
of Jesus in meditation in which he came to her without
form. Her monastic superiors expressed concern about
the experience, thinking that it was heretical—then they
discovered a teaching by an early Christian saint that the
experience of Christ's consciousness beyond form is the
highest experience of him.

God is infinitely vast and beyond all forms, but He is
also in the forms in which we worship him. He can be
known in form or beyond form. The devotee can worship
the Divine in whatever way his natural inclination takes
him. In a wonderful chant, Ram Prasad, a Bengali householder saint, said, "Thousands of *Vedas* [scriptures] say that
Divine Mother is without form; but come to me as the
Mother whom I hold most dear."

Self-offering

Yogananda repeatedly emphasized the importance of
self-offering. What we *receive* in meditation, including visions
and phenomena, are not nearly as important as what we *give*.
What matters most is the complete self-offering of ourselves
to God. This is how we become absorbed in His love.

Selflessness and self-offering are the surest paths to divine freedom. When we practice any form of meditation selfishly, including the highest technique of Kriya Yoga, our practice can strengthen the ego's hold. The best results are attained by humble, childlike devotional self-offering in prayer, meditation, and while practicing the techniques. Selfless service, *seva*, is one powerful form of self-offering.

When the experience of *samadhi* comes, then giving and receiving become merged in divine union. As Yogananda put in his great mystical poem, *Samadhi*, "Thou art I, I am Thou, Knowing, Knower, Known, as One!"

Pray and Meditate in God

Until the experience of divine union comes, it can help to visualize or feel that there is no separation between us and God. Try to feel that we are *in* God, and God is in us. Merging in God can be visualized as a gradual progression, even as Patanjali describes the four highest states of the eight-limbed path of yoga: interiorization of the mind and life force (*pratyahara*); concentration on God or one of His aspects (*dharana*); meditation in God (*dhyana*); complete absorption and union with God (*samadhi*).

Of the many ways we can develop in inner communion, of special importance to Kriya Yogis is communing with God as the cosmic sound of creation, AUM. Yogananda gave a specific technique to help people become absorbed in that cosmic vibration.*

---

* You can read more about this technique in Joseph Bharat Cornell's book *AUM: The Melody of Love*, published by Crystal Clarity Publishers.

The time for knowing God has come. Kriya Yoga is a spiritual practice that will take us to the actual perception of God. If you don't pick up the cloth of Kriya by the right thread, it will unravel over time. But when practiced with devotion and deep attention, Kriya has the power to bring us to the divine experience, to turn ordinary people into saints. I have seen firsthand the proof of Yogananda's promise:

> I can take a few young men of the most restless sort and let them practice Kriya for two hours every day in the way I tell them, and, without question, in four or five years I can make saints out of them.
>
> I won't preach a single sermon to them. I will simply tell them to practice Kriya for two hours a day, and they will see the difference in their lives. That is a good challenge.
>
> Of course, they must practice in the way that I tell them. That won't be easy. But it is surely worth the effort.

— PARAMHANSA YOGANANDA, *The Essence of Self-Realization*

In the end, words and theory can only hint at the divine experience. Always remember: those who make the right kind of effort will find the fulfillment of all their wishes—a fulfillment that comes only with the taste of the Divine.

While it is true that only God's grace can free us, we can never attain divine freedom if we await it passively. The miracle of salvation comes only to those who hold their hearts consciously open to God, and who entertain deep love for Him—who do not believe in God only with their minds, but receive Him in their hearts, into the darkest corners of their being.

Eventually, by deep, inner communion with the divine light, the darkness will be banished from your consciousness. When at last it vanishes, it will leave you forever, as though it had never been!

— SWAMI KRIYANANDA, *Rays of the Same Light*

CHAPTER SEVENTEEN

The Final Exam

Prepare yourself for the coming astral journey of death by daily riding in the balloon of God-perception. Through delusion you are perceiving yourself as a bundle of flesh and bones, which at best is a nest of troubles.

— PARAMHANSA YOGANANDA, *Autobiography of a Yogi*

have had the odd good fortune to experience a number of close calls with death. They were good fortune, because none of them ended my life, and because I learned beautiful lessons. One close encounter occurred a few months after I had begun to follow Paramhansa Yogananda. I described it in a compilation of similar experiences of many people, published by Asha Nayaswami, titled *Loved and Protected*:

I vaguely remember that there was a sign saying: "Dangerous Currents. No Lifeguard." I grew up in the middle of the United States. At age twenty I had hardly ever seen an ocean and certainly knew very little about them, so the sign meant nothing to me. It was a beautiful sunny day, and there I was in California at the Pacific Ocean. All I could think about was diving into those waves.

Paddling around in the water, I reveled in this new experience. Then everything changed. I was caught in a rip tide, and it was carrying me away from shore. I fought against it, but the current was too strong. Farther and farther it took me out into the sea, until the crashing surf was tossing me about like a rag doll.

I struggled and struggled to no avail. I was fighting for my life and the ocean was winning. Finally, unable to swim another stroke, I turned over onto my back and literally went "belly up." I was convinced there was nothing I could do and no one who could save me.

Waves were crashing around me, but I felt completely calm. I had never considered what I would do when faced with death. In hindsight, I am surprised by my response. I had just started meditating recently, and I knew God was out there somewhere. I wasn't sure, though, what role he might play in my life, and what my relationship was to him.

Now, as I looked at the vast blue sky, the bright sun, and the ocean around me, I offered myself completely to God. No words. I wasn't asking to be saved. I didn't pray to die quickly. With all my heart, I just gave myself back to Him.

What happened next seemed the most natural thing in the world. In response to my self-offering, God gave me bliss. Self-offering equals bliss: It is a lesson I have never forgotten.

Basking in this bliss, it took me a few minutes to realize that I was now floating in calm water. I rested there until my strength returned. Then I dog-paddled in a channel of calm water all the way back to shore.

I believe that God was giving me a foretaste of the eventual, inevitable passing from this life, perhaps to reassure me that the moment would not be too difficult and might even be filled with bliss. Most importantly, God was showing me the attitude that we should cultivate toward what Swami Kriyananda called The Final Exam.*

In the last years of his life, Kriyananda seemed to be living continuously in a radiant inner state of divine bliss, even as his body was failing him. During those final years, a friend went to Kriyananda's home in Pune, India. He was eating dinner after giving a public lecture to a large audience. My friend was taken aback to see him so weak that he could barely lift the fork to his mouth.

My friend later admitted how embarrassed he'd been, when a thought flashed in his mind that in private, Kriyananda didn't seem to have the same high energy that he

---

* There is an entire chapter entitled "The Final Exam" in Swami Kriyananda's book *Religion in the New Age* published by Crystal Clarity Publishers.

spoke of in public. Catching my friend's thought, Kriyananda slowly turned and looked up at him, then spoke with deep energy: "On the inside, perfect joy!" Quietly, then, he went back to his meal, and my friend's doubts were dissolved.

We cannot hold on to our bodies forever. If we live to a ripe old age, the body may become a burden. Relying for our happiness on our physical well-being—or simply on the absence of pain—is to set ourselves up to suffer. But if we have lived a life in God—a life of love, kindness, and selflessness—then we will have fed an inner joy that will only grow as we age.

To borrow a financial term, our body is a "depreciating asset," much like an old house that has seen better days. The value of the human body will inevitably depreciate until it is reduced to dust or ashes, according to how we choose to dispose of the remains. While we are living, we should do everything in our power to keep the body strong and healthy. Yogananda advised us to "keep the body fit for God-realization." I've seen how Kriya Yogis who ignore the guru's advice to exercise daily seem to lose their inner balance, and that they often have greater difficulties with their spiritual life.

At the same time, if you invest *all* your most valuable resources—time, energy, passion—into that depreciating asset, the body, you will be making a poor investment. The body is bound to let you down. How, then, should we live to prepare ourselves for the Final Exam? Let us look at some helpful attitudes and practices.

First, understand that, even now, we are very close to knowing God. Although we cannot know how close we are, if the yearning for God is there, we can trust that we are approaching the end of a journey of many lifetimes. How close? "God," Yogananda said, "is just behind your thoughts, just behind your feelings."

When I lived at Ananda Village, I would make frequent trips around the world to share Yogananda's teachings. It wasn't always easy to leave the beautiful environment and go out "into the world."

When I returned from those travels, which were often exhausting, the final stage of the journey was a short drive from the airport to Ananda Village. At the time, the final stretch of road led past a decrepit old barn that was easily over a century old. It was situated no more than a half-mile before we reached the Ananda property. The sides of the barn had more holes than wood, and the frame was barely able to hold it upright. Trees grew inside the barn and poked their leafy branches through gaping holes in the roof.

I heard some Ananda friends discuss whether they should ask the neighbor to tear down the barn, since it was an eyesore. I had to stop myself from pleading, "No! Please don't tear down that barn!" I was thinking of how, whenever I returned from a trip, I would see the ruined barn and my heart would leap with joy, Ananda (which means divine bliss) is just behind that barn! I'm almost there!"

I try to recall that feeling when I meditate. The act of trying to meditate, of struggling with our restless thoughts and feelings, is in itself reason for hope and positive expectation. We can trust that God is *just behind* our restless thoughts — that we are very, very close, and getting closer every day.

In the lives of several close friends, I have seen how God has withheld the final experience of freedom in Him until the very end. Perhaps He chose to withhold the experience because they had work to complete in the world, or people to help. Whatever the reason, and however long it takes, our part is simply to trust, and to keep moving forward as best we can. The grace of God will take care of the rest.

I've also found it helpful—whatever we are doing and wherever we go—always to be looking for God. We may not see Him directly, but I have found that the effort begins to dissolve the veil that separates us from God.

Paramhansa Yogananda used the analogy of a movie theater. Before movies were shown digitally, the image on the screen came from a light projected from a booth at the back of the theater. Similarly, Yogananda explained that just as the movie of this life seems real to us, it is merely a play of light and shadow on "the screen of duality." He urged his disciples to follow the beam of light from the screen back to the projection booth. In this way, we can glimpse the One who is putting on the show of creation, including our own life.

Meditation follows the same principle: it enables us to penetrate the superficial drama of this world and to concentrate on the beam of light that is emanating from God and projecting everything we see. In this way, the meditator can travel along the beam of light through his thoughts and feelings and consciousness, past this dream existence, to the One who is dreaming everything into existence.

I like to view my daily life as a game of hide-and-seek with God. "I know that You are hiding everywhere! I am going to keep looking for You wherever I go. Where will I see You today?" By following this practice, you will begin to catch glimpses of God, often in surprising places.

Here is a final story, which illustrates the fruits of this practice. I was boarding a flight after leading an inspiring weekend Kriya retreat. At the time, I was dealing with chronic pain that made traveling difficult. On its way to California, the flight would stop at the Las Vegas airport. The thought of going from a spiritually uplifting retreat into a plane full of partygoers, some of them already fueled up with alcohol, made me feel even more weary.

I prayed to Divine Mother, "I know you are here somewhere. Please, please show Yourself to me on this trip. I need Your comfort and some proof that You are guiding and loving me."

I know it was a childish prayer, but that is what my heart spoke. I had three very clear responses to my prayer that day. I'll share one of them with you.

As soon as the plane took off, a small baby, just a few seats behind me, began crying—screaming really. During the entire flight the baby only stopped screaming when it needed to take a deep breath, before letting out another blast. I tried to listen intuitively to why the infant was crying.

As I listened, I felt that I could hear through the screams the baby's soul calling out, "Where am I? How did I get here? This is so different from the beautiful place that I just came from!" Nothing could satisfy that cry.

I was tempted to get up from my seat and whisper in the newborn's ear, "That's right, this isn't your true home. You will have to do everything you can to bring that light and love of Home into this world. Your parents and friends will try to distract you at times and make you forget. They will dangle bright shiny objects in front of you and offer larger shiny toys as you grow older—all to make you forget the purpose of your life. Whatever you do, don't forget! Keep crying to your Divine Parents as you are now! Never stop calling to Them. They will respond!"

I'm speaking to that child in all of us. If we try always to remember, and to spend more time with others who are remembering God, we will not forget. I confess that I enjoyed listening to the baby screaming during that flight, which lasted several hours. It was a reminder to me to never stop calling to God.

If we can spend this life looking for God, calling to God, giving, serving, loving, and being instruments of light into the world, we will pass the Final Exam. If we live in the right way even now, we don't have to wait for the Final Moment to feel the bliss of our own nature.

A very good attitude to have when difficulties and trials come to you suddenly is: "God, my life is in your hands." Try to develop that attitude by practicing over a period of time until you can come up with it instantly. It's very helpful to imagine the worst.

God will give you joy if you live in Him and even if calamities come to you, His blessing will be there. People who leave their bodies with God in their hearts don't suffer; any pain they might feel is minimized or non-existent. Those who die thinking of God or for God, like a Joan of Arc, go in bliss.

If in the face of death itself you feel joy, that itself is a great victory. All victory depends upon being in tune with God, the source of all truth. So, try to love in a divine, unconditional way as much as possible.

— SWAMI KRIYANANDA, "DEVOTION: YOUR PROTECTION IN DIFFICULT TIMES," *Clarity Magazine*, WINTER 2008

Appendix:
How to Learn Kriya Yoga
through Ananda Sangha

Ananda Sangha teaches Kriya Yoga just as Paramhansa Yogananda taught it. Kriya is a technique, and it is an entire approach to life. The Kriya technique is part of a comprehensive spiritual path that includes three other techniques (Energization Exercises, *Hong-Sau*, AUM Meditation), along with discipleship to the Kriya line of Gurus.

The Kriya technique is taught through initiation by an Ananda Kriyacharya (a Kriya Yoga teacher). There is an unbroken link from Mahavatar Babaji, through Lahiri Mahasaya, Swami Sri Yukteswar, Paramhansa Yogananda, and his disciple Swami Kriyananda, to all Ananda kriyacharyas. The kriyacharya is authorized by the spiritual director of Ananda Sangha to initiate people into Kriya. The kriyacharya is not a guru, but acts as an instrument for the Ananda line of gurus.

Before you can be initiated into Kriya Yoga, there is a process of study and preparation. It includes study of Paramhansa Yogananda's teachings and establishing a daily meditation practice using techniques that are part of the Kriya path. This process can take nine months to one year, sometimes longer, depending on the individual. Again, this is just as Paramhansa Yogananda wished Kriya Yogis to prepare to receive the Kriya technique.

The preparatory courses can be studied in-person, through online classes, book study, or a combination of these. Regardless of whether you choose to learn in-person or online, you will receive personal spiritual support, resources, and many opportunities to ask questions of our experienced meditation teachers. After learning Kriya Yoga, Ananda continues to offer ongoing support and guidance in your spiritual practices.

Ananda Sangha has prepared thousands of people for Kriya initiation over the last fifty-five years.

We give Kriya initiations most frequently in the United States, India, and Italy. Our teachers also travel to other countries including Mexico, Russia, Singapore, Australia, New Zealand, and others to give initiations.

To learn more, contact:

Ananda Sangha Worldwide   **kriyayoga@ananda.org**

Ananda India   **kriyasupport@anandaindia.org**

Ananda Europa   **kriyayoga@ananda.it**

Find Ananda Near You   **ananda.org/find-ananda/**

References

Devi, Vanamali. 2012. *The Complete Life of Krishna: Based on the Earliest Oral Traditions and the Sacred Scriptures.* Rochester: Inner Traditions.

Hermanns, William. 1983. *Einstein and the Poet: In Search of the Cosmic Man.* Wellesley: Branden Books.

Kriyananda, Swami. 2004. *Conversations with Yogananda.* Commerce: Crystal Clarity Publishers.

Kriyananda, Swami. 2013. *Demystifying Patanjali.* Commerce: Crystal Clarity Publishers.

Kriyananda, Swami. 1999. *The Light of Superconsciousness.* Commerce: Crystal Clarity Publishers.

Kriyananda, Swami. 2009. *The New Path.* Commerce: Crystal Clarity Publishers.

Kriyananda, Swami. 2012. *Paramhansa Yogananda: A Biography.* Commerce: Crystal Clarity Publishers.

Kriyananda, Swami. 2004. *A Place Called Ananda.* Commerce: Crystal Clarity Publishers.

Kriyananda, Swami. 2009. *Religion in the New Age.* Commerce: Crystal Clarity Publishers.

Kriyananda, Swami. 2010. *A Renunciate Order for the New Age.* Commerce: Crystal Clarity Publishers.

Kriyananda, Swami. 1973. *The Road Ahead*. Commerce: Crystal Clarity Publishers.

Monnin, Alfred. 1862. *Life of the Curé D'ars*. London: Burns & Lambert.

Selbie, Joseph and David Steinmetz. 2010. *The Yugas*. Commerce: Crystal Clarity Publishers.

Sri Yukteswar, Swami. 1990. *The Holy Science*. Los Angeles: Self-Realization Fellowship.

Yogananda, Paramhansa. 1936. *Original Praecepta Lessons*.

Yogananda, Paramhansa. 1938. *Cosmic Chants*. Los Angeles: Self-Realization Fellowship.

Yogananda, Paramhansa. 1940. "When I Am Only a Dream."

Yogananda, Paramhansa. 1994. *Autobiography of a Yogi*. 1946 Original ed. Commerce: Crystal Clarity Publishers.

Yogananda, Paramhansa. 1990. *The Essence of Self-Realization*. Commerce: Crystal Clarity Publishers.

Yogananda, Paramhansa. 2008. *How to Be a Success*. Commerce: Crystal Clarity Publishers.

About the Author

NAYASWAMI DEVARSHI is a long-time Ananda minister and *Kriyacharya* (authorized Kriya Yoga teacher). He currently lives in India, leading the Ananda monastery, and serving as the director of Ananda's Global Kriya Yoga Sangha. Devarshi works with those taking Kriya Yoga for the first time, and counsels long-time practitioners. He prepares devotees to receive Kriya Yoga and conducts Kriya Initiations in India and South America.

About Paramhansa Yogananda

"As a bright light shining in the midst of darkness, so was Yogananda's presence in this world. Such a great soul comes on earth only rarely, when there is a real need among men."

—His Holiness the Shankaracharya
of Kanchipuram

Born in 1893, Yogananda was the first yoga master of India to take up permanent residence in the West.

Yogananda arrived in America in 1920 and traveled throughout the country on what he called his "spiritual campaigns." Hundreds of thousands filled the largest halls in major cities to see the yoga master from India. Yogananda continued to lecture and write up to his passing in 1952.

Yogananda's initial impact on Western culture was truly impressive. His lasting spiritual legacy has been even greater. His *Autobiography of a Yogi*, first published in 1946, helped launch a spiritual revolution in the West. Translated into more than fifty languages, it remains a best-selling spiritual classic to this day.

Before embarking on his mission, Yogananda received this admonition from his teacher, Swami Sri Yukteswar: "The West is high in material attainments but lacking in spiritual understanding. It is God's will that you play a role in teaching mankind the value of balancing the material with an inner, spiritual life."

In addition to *Autobiography of a Yogi*, Yogananda's spiritual legacy includes music, poetry, and extensive commentaries on the Bhagavad Gita, the *Rubaiyat* of Omar Khayyam, and the Christian Bible, showing the principles of Self-realization as the unifying truth underlying all true religions. Through his teachings and his Kriya Yoga path millions of people around the world have found a new way to connect personally with God.

His mission, however, was far broader than all this. It was to help usher the whole world into Dwapara Yuga, the new Age of Energy in which we live. "Someday," Swami Kriyananda wrote, "I believe he will be seen as the *avatar* of Dwapara Yuga: the way shower for a new age."

FURTHER EXPLORATIONS

CRYSTAL CLARITY PUBLISHERS

If you enjoyed this title, Crystal Clarity Publishers invites you to deepen your spiritual life through many additional resources based on the teachings of Paramhansa Yogananda. We offer books, e-books, audiobooks, yoga and meditation videos, and a wide variety of inspirational and relaxation music composed by Swami Kriyananda.

See a listing of books below, visit our secure website for a complete online catalog, or place an order for our products.

crystalclarity.com

800.424.1055 | clarity@crystalclarity.com

1123 Goodrich Blvd. | Commerce, CA 90022

ANANDA WORLDWIDE

Crystal Clarity Publishers is the publishing house of Ananda, a worldwide spiritual movement founded by Swami Kriyananda, a direct disciple of Paramhansa Yogananda. Ananda offers resources and support for your spiritual journey through meditation instruction, webinars, online virtual community, email, and chat.

Ananda has more than 150 centers and meditation groups in over 45 countries, offering group guided meditations, classes and teacher training in meditation and yoga, and many other resources.

In addition, Ananda has developed eight residential communities in the US, Europe, and India. Spiritual communities are places where people live together in a spirit of cooperation and friendship, dedicated to a common goal. Spirituality is practiced in all areas of daily life: at school, at work, or in the home. Many Ananda communities offer internships during which one can stay and experience spiritual community firsthand.

For more information about Ananda communities or meditation groups near you, please visit **ananda.org** or call 530.478.7560.

THE EXPANDING LIGHT RETREAT

The Expanding Light is the largest retreat center in the world to share exclusively the teachings of Paramhansa Yogananda. Situated in the Ananda Village community near Nevada City, California, the center offers the opportunity to experience spiritual life in a contemporary ashram setting. The varied, year-round schedule of classes and programs on yoga, meditation, and spiritual practice includes Karma Yoga, personal retreat, spiritual travel, and online learning. Large groups are welcome.

The Ananda School of Yoga & Meditation offers certified yoga, yoga therapist, spiritual counselor, and meditation teacher trainings.

The teaching staff has years of experience practicing Kriya Yoga meditation and all aspects of Paramhansa Yogananda's teachings. You may come for a relaxed personal renewal, participating in ongoing activities as much or as little as you wish. The serene mountain setting, supportive staff, and delicious vegetarian meals provide an ideal environment for a truly meaningful stay, be it a brief respite or an extended spiritual vacation.

For more information, please visit **expandinglight.org** or call 800.346.5350.

ANANDA MEDITATION RETREAT

Set amidst seventy-two acres of beautiful meditation gardens and wild forest in Northern California's Sierra foothills, the Ananda Meditation Retreat is an ideal setting for a rejuvenating, inner experience.

The Meditation Retreat has been a place of deep meditation and sincere devotion for over fifty years. Long before that, the Native American Maidu tribe held this to be sacred land. The beauty and presence of the Divine are tangibly felt by all who visit here.

Studies show that being in nature and using techniques such as forest bathing can significantly reduce stress and blood pressure while strengthening your immune system, concentration, and level of happiness. The Meditation Retreat is the perfect place for quiet immersion in nature.

Plan a personal retreat, enjoy one of the guided retreats, or choose from a variety of programs led by the caring and joyful staff.

For more information or to place your reservation, please visit **meditationretreat.org**, email **meditationretreat@ananda.org**, or call 530.478.7557.

THE ORIGINAL WRITINGS OF PARAMHANSA YOGANANDA

THE 1946 UNEDITED EDITION OF PARAMHANSA YOGANANDA'S SPIRITUAL MASTERPIECE

AUTOBIOGRAPHY OF A YOGI
Paramhansa Yogananda

Autobiography of a Yogi is one of the world's most acclaimed spiritual classics, with millions of copies sold. Named one of the Best 100 Spiritual Books of the twentieth century, this book helped launch and continues to inspire a spiritual awakening throughout the Western world.

Yogananda was the first yoga master of India whose mission brought him to settle and teach in the West. His firsthand account of his life experiences in India includes childhood revelations, stories of his visits to saints and masters, and long-secret teachings of yoga and Self-realization that he first made available to the Western reader.

This reprint of the original 1946 edition is free from textual changes made after Yogananda's passing in 1952. This updated edition includes bonus materials: the last chapter that Yogananda wrote in 1951, also without posthumous changes, the eulogy Yogananda wrote for Gandhi, and a new foreword and afterword by Swami Kriyananda, one of Yogananda's close, direct disciples.

Also available in Spanish and Hindi from Crystal Clarity Publishers.

SCIENTIFIC HEALING AFFIRMATIONS
Paramhansa Yogananda

Yogananda's 1924 classic, reprinted here, is a pioneering work in the fields of self-healing and self-transformation. He explains that words are crystallized thoughts and have life-changing power when spoken with conviction, concentration, willpower, and feeling. Yogananda offers far more than mere suggestions for achieving positive attitudes. He shows how to impregnate words with spiritual force to shift habitual thought patterns of the mind and create a new personal reality.

Added to this text are over fifty of Yogananda's well-loved "Short Affirmations," taken from issues of *East-West* and *Inner Culture* magazines from 1932 to 1942. This little book will be a treasured companion on the road to realizing your highest, divine potential.

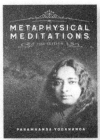

METAPHYSICAL MEDITATIONS
Paramhansa Yogananda

Metaphysical Meditations is a classic collection of meditation techniques, visualizations, affirmations, and prayers from the great yoga master, Paramhansa Yogananda. The meditations given are of three types: those spoken to the individual consciousness, prayers or demands addressed to God, and affirmations that bring us closer to the Divine.

Select a passage that meets your specific need and speak each word slowly and purposefully until you become absorbed in its inner meaning. At the bedside, by the meditation seat, or while traveling—one can choose no better companion than *Metaphysical Meditations*.

THE WISDOM OF YOGANANDA *series*

Paramhansa Yogananda's timeless wisdom is offered here in an approachable, easy-to-read format. The writings of the Master are presented with minimal editing to capture his expansive and compassionate wisdom, his sense of fun, and his practical spiritual guidance.

HOW TO BE HAPPY ALL THE TIME
The Wisdom of Yogananda, volume 1

Yogananda explains everything needed to lead a happier, more fulfilling life. Topics include: looking for happiness in the right places; choosing to be happy; tools, techniques, and methods for achieving happiness; sharing happiness with others; and balancing success with happiness.

KARMA AND REINCARNATION
The Wisdom of Yogananda, volume 2

Yogananda reveals the reality of karma, death, reincarnation, and the afterlife. With clarity and simplicity, he makes the mysterious understandable: why we see a world of suffering and inequality; what happens at death and after death; the purpose of reincarnation; and how to handle the challenges we face in our lives.

HOW TO LOVE AND BE LOVED
The Wisdom of Yogananda, volume 3

Yogananda shares practical guidance and fresh insight on relationships of all types: how to cure friendship-ending habits; how to choose the right partner; the role of sex in marriage; how to conceive a spiritually oriented child; the solutions to problems that arise in marriage; and the Universal Love at the heart of all relationships.

HOW TO BE A SUCCESS
The Wisdom of Yogananda, volume 4

The Attributes of Success, Yogananda's original booklet on reaching one's goals, is included here along with his other writings on success: how to develop habits of success and eradicate habits of failure; thriving in the right job; how to build willpower and magnetism; and finding the true purpose of one's life.

HOW TO HAVE COURAGE, CALMNESS, AND CONFIDENCE
The Wisdom of Yogananda, volume 5

A master at helping people change and grow, Yogananda shows how to transform one's life: dislodge negative thoughts and depression; uproot fear and thoughts of failure; cure nervousness and systematically eliminate worry from life; and overcome anger, sorrow, oversensitivity, and a host of other troublesome emotions.

Winner of the 2011 International Book Award for Best Self-Help Title

HOW TO ACHIEVE GLOWING HEALTH AND VITALITY
The Wisdom of Yogananda, volume 6

Yogananda explains principles that promote physical health and overall well-being, mental clarity, and inspiration in one's spiritual life. He offers practical, wide-ranging, and fascinating suggestions on having more energy and living a radiantly healthy life. Readers will discover the priceless Energization Exercises for rejuvenating the body and mind, the fine art of conscious relaxation, and helpful diet tips for health and beauty.

HOW TO AWAKEN YOUR TRUE POTENTIAL
The Wisdom of Yogananda, volume 7

With compassion, humor, and deep understanding of human psychology, Yogananda offers instruction on releasing limitations to access the power of mind and heart. Discover your hidden resources and be empowered to choose a life with greater meaning, purpose, and joy.

THE MAN WHO REFUSED HEAVEN
The Wisdom of Yogananda, volume 8

Why is humor so deeply appreciated? Laughter is one of the great joys of life. Joy is fundamental to who we are. The humor in this book is taken from Yogananda's writings. Also included are experiences with the Master that demonstrate his playful spirit.

HOW TO FACE LIFE'S CHANGES
The Wisdom of Yogananda, volume 9

Changes come not to destroy us, but to help us grow in understanding and learn the lessons we must to reach our highest potential. Guided by Yogananda, tap into the changeless joy of your soul-nature, empowering you to move through life fearlessly and with an open heart. Learn to accept change as the reality of life; face change in relationships, finances, and health with gratitude; and cultivate key attitudes like fearlessness, non-attachment, and willpower.

HOW TO SPIRITUALIZE YOUR LIFE
The Wisdom of Yogananda, volume 10

Yogananda addresses financial, physical, mental, emotional, and spiritual challenges, he explains how best to expand one's consciousness and live life to the fullest. Compiled from his articles, lessons, and handwritten letters, this tenth volume in the Wisdom of Yogananda series was written in a question-and-answer format, well suited to both individual and group study.

HOW TO LIVE WITHOUT FEAR
The Wisdom of Yogananda, volume 11

Releases: March 2024

MOMENTS OF TRUTH, VOLUME ONE
Excerpts from the Rubaiyat of Omar Khayyam Explained
Paramhansa Yogananda

"One day, as I was deeply concentrated on the pages of Omar Khayyam's *Rubaiyat*, I suddenly beheld the walls of its outer meanings crumble away. Lo! vast inner meanings opened like a golden treasure house before my gaze."
—Paramhansa Yogananda

Moments of Truth, Volume One is the first in a series of small books of excerpts from the teachings of Paramhansa Yogananda, as set forth in his own books and in those of his close disciple, Swami Kriyananda.

The gems of wisdom in this little volume are taken from Yogananda's commentaries on *The Rubaiyat of Omar Khayyam*, considered by Westerners a celebration of earthly pleasures, but widely recognized in the East as a work of profound spirituality. Yogananda's commentaries are a true scripture in their own right. These selections have scripture's power to change your consciousness, and your life.

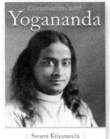

Swami Kriyananda

CONVERSATIONS WITH YOGANANDA
Stories, Sayings, and Wisdom of Paramhansa Yogananda
Recorded with reflections, by his disciple, Swami Kriyananda

For those who enjoyed Paramhansa Yogananda's autobiography and long for more, this collection of conversations offers rare intimate glimpses of life with the Master as never before shared.

This is an unparalleled account of Yogananda and his teachings written by one of his foremost disciples. Swami Kriyananda was often present when Yogananda spoke privately with other close disciples, received visitors and answered their questions, and dictated and discussed his writings. He recorded the Master's words, preserving a treasure trove of wisdom that would otherwise have been lost.

These Conversations include not only Yogananda's words as he spoke them, but the added insight of a disciple who spent over fifty years attuning his consciousness to that of his guru.

The collection features nearly five hundred stories, sayings, and insights from the twentieth century's most famous master of yoga, as well as twenty-five photos—nearly all previously unreleased.

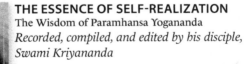

THE ESSENCE OF SELF-REALIZATION
The Wisdom of Paramhansa Yogananda
Recorded, compiled, and edited by his disciple,
Swami Kriyananda

Filled with lessons, stories, and jewels of wisdom that Paramhansa Yogananda shared only with his closest disciples, this volume is an invaluable guide to the spiritual life, carefully organized in twenty main topics.

Great teachers work through their students, and Yogananda was no exception. Swami Kriyananda comments, "After I'd been with him a year and a half, he began urging me to write down the things he was saying during informal conversations." Many of the three hundred sayings presented here are available nowhere else. This book and *Conver-*

sations with Yogananda are must-reads for anyone wishing to know more about Yogananda's teachings and to absorb his wisdom.

"Be assured that at each sitting, whether for one page or one chapter, you will have gleaned some refreshment for a tired heart or a thirsty soul. . . . *Essence* is easy to read, besides being quite a bit of fun."

— *Spirit of Change Magazine*

THE ESSENCE OF THE BHAGAVAD GITA
Explained by Paramhansa Yogananda
As remembered by his disciple, Swami Kriyananda

Rarely in a lifetime does a new spiritual classic appear that has the power to change people's lives and transform future generations. This is such a book. This revelation of India's best-loved scripture approaches it from a fresh perspective, showing its deep allegorical meaning and down-to-earth practicality. The themes presented are universal: how to achieve victory in life through union with the Divine; how to prepare for life's final exam — death — and what happens afterward; and how to triumph over all pain and suffering.

Swami Kriyananda worked with Paramhansa Yogananda in 1950 while the Master completed his commentary. At that time, Yogananda commissioned him to disseminate his teachings worldwide.

"Millions will find God through this book!" Yogananda declared upon completion of the manuscript. "Not just thousands — millions. I have seen it. I know."

GOD AS DIVINE MOTHER
Wisdom and Inspiration for Love and Acceptance
Paramhansa Yogananda and Swami Kriyananda

We long for a God who loves us exactly as we are, who doesn't judge us but rather helps and encourages us in achieving our highest potential. In this book, discover the teachings and inspirations on Divine Mother from Paramhansa Yogananda. These teachings are universal: No matter your religious background, or lack thereof, you will find these messages of love and acceptance resonating on a soul-level. Included also are over thirty poems and prayers dedicated to God in the form of Divine Mother, and original chants and songs by the authors.

The gems of wisdom in this little volume are taken from Yogananda's commentaries on *The Rubaiyat of Omar Khayyam*, considered by Westerners a celebration of earthly pleasures, but widely recognized in the East as a work of profound spirituality. Yogananda's commentaries are a true scripture in their own right. These selections have scripture's power to change your consciousness, and your life.

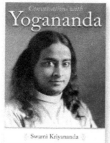

Swami Kriyananda

CONVERSATIONS WITH YOGANANDA
Stories, Sayings, and Wisdom of Paramhansa Yogananda
Recorded with reflections, by his disciple, Swami Kriyananda

For those who enjoyed Paramhansa Yogananda's autobiography and long for more, this collection of conversations offers rare intimate glimpses of life with the Master as never before shared.

This is an unparalleled account of Yogananda and his teachings written by one of his foremost disciples. Swami Kriyananda was often present when Yogananda spoke privately with other close disciples, received visitors and answered their questions, and dictated and discussed his writings. He recorded the Master's words, preserving a treasure trove of wisdom that would otherwise have been lost.

These Conversations include not only Yogananda's words as he spoke them, but the added insight of a disciple who spent over fifty years attuning his consciousness to that of his guru.

The collection features nearly five hundred stories, sayings, and insights from the twenthieth century's most famous master of yoga, as well as twenty-five photos—nearly all previously unreleased.

THE ESSENCE OF SELF-REALIZATION
The Wisdom of Paramhansa Yogananda
Recorded, compiled, and edited by his disciple,
Swami Kriyananda

Filled with lessons, stories, and jewels of wisdom that Paramhansa Yogananda shared only with his closest disciples, this volume is an invaluable guide to the spiritual life, carefully organized in twenty main topics.

Great teachers work through their students, and Yogananda was no exception. Swami Kriyananda comments, "After I'd been with him a year and a half, he began urging me to write down the things he was saying during informal conversations." Many of the three hundred sayings presented here are available nowhere else. This book and *Conver-*

sations with Yogananda are must-reads for anyone wishing to know more about Yogananda's teachings and to absorb his wisdom.

"Be assured that at each sitting, whether for one page or one chapter, you will have gleaned some refreshment for a tired heart or a thirsty soul. . . . *Essence* is easy to read, besides being quite a bit of fun."

— Spirit of Change Magazine

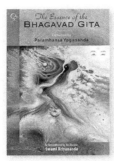

THE ESSENCE OF THE BHAGAVAD GITA
Explained by Paramhansa Yogananda
As remembered by his disciple, Swami Kriyananda

Rarely in a lifetime does a new spiritual classic appear that has the power to change people's lives and transform future generations. This is such a book. This revelation of India's best-loved scripture approaches it from a fresh perspective, showing its deep allegorical meaning and down-to-earth practicality. The themes presented are universal: how to achieve victory in life through union with the Divine; how to prepare for life's final exam—death—and what happens afterward; and how to triumph over all pain and suffering.

Swami Kriyananda worked with Paramhansa Yogananda in 1950 while the Master completed his commentary. At that time, Yogananda commissioned him to disseminate his teachings worldwide.

"Millions will find God through this book!" Yogananda declared upon completion of the manuscript. "Not just thousands—millions. I have seen it. I know."

GOD AS DIVINE MOTHER
Wisdom and Inspiration for Love and Acceptance
Paramhansa Yogananda and Swami Kriyananda

We long for a God who loves us exactly as we are, who doesn't judge us but rather helps and encourages us in achieving our highest potential. In this book, discover the teachings and inspirations on Divine Mother from Paramhansa Yogananda. These teachings are universal: No matter your religious background, or lack thereof, you will find these messages of love and acceptance resonating on a soul-level. Included also are over thirty poems and prayers dedicated to God in the form of Divine Mother, and original chants and songs by the authors.

"The role of the Divine Mother is to draw all Her children, all self-aware beings everywhere, back to oneness with God."

In this book, you will discover: Who is Divine Mother?; How to develop the heart's natural love; What attitudes draw Her grace; How to tune in to Divine Mother. Included also are over thirty poems and prayers dedicated to God in the form of Divine Mother, as well as original chants and songs by the authors.

MORE SELECTED OFFERINGS

Wisdom Stories series
Paramhansa Yogananda
    Stories from India, volume 1
    Stories from India, volume 2

For Starters series
    Meditation for Starters *by Swami Kriyananda*
    Intuition for Starters *by Swami Kriyananda*
    Chakras for Starters *by Savitri Simpson*
    Vegetarian Cooking for Starters *by Diksha McCord*

Secrets series
Swami Kriyananda
    Meditation and Inner Peace
    Success and Leadership
    Health and Healing
    Spiritualizing Your Daily Life

Touch of Light series
Nayaswami Jyotish and Nayaswami Devi
    Touch of Light • Touch of Joy
    Touch of Love • Touch of Peace
    Touch of Divine Wisdom (2023)

Affirmations for Self-Healing
Swami Kriyananda

The Art and Science of Raja Yoga
Swami Kriyananda

Art As a Hidden Message
Swami Kriyananda

AUM: The Melody of Love
Joseph Bharat Cornell

Change Your Magnetism, Change Your Life
Naidhruva Rush

Divine Will Healing
Mary Kretzmann

Eastern Thoughts, Western Thoughts
Swami Kriyananda

The Essential Flower Essence Handbook
Lila Devi

The Flawless Mirror
Kamala Silva

Flow Learning
Joseph Bharat Cornell

The Four Stages of Yoga
Nischala Cryer

God Is for Everyone
Inspired by Paramhansa Yogananda
As taught to and understood by his disciple, Swami Kriyananda

The Harmonium Handbook
Satyaki Kraig Brockschmidt

A Healer's Handbook
Mary Kretzmann

Healing Kitchen
Diksha McCord

How to Meditate
Jyotish Novak

In Divine Friendship
Swami Kriyananda

The Joyful Athlete
George Beinhorn

Lightbearer
Asha Nayaswami

The Meaning of Dreaming
Savitri Simpson

My Heart Remembers
Narayani Anaya

CPSIA information can be obtained
at www.ICGtesting.com
Printed in the USA
LVHW081327030523
745940LV00006B/10